PRAISE FOR *TEACHIN*

The engaged and engaging writing style of this textbook—with its clear, concise definitions and discussions springing from conversations, dialogues, and self-reflections—inspires readers to reflect on and reinvigorate their teaching in dynamic ways.

Teaching From the Heart touches on the core issues involved in critical communication pedagogy in today's world and provides the reader with a wealth of resources and activities to become a critical teacher.

—Armeda Celestine Reitzel, Professor and Chair, Humboldt State University

Teaching From the Heart takes something that seems ideal just in theory—getting students to open up about their feelings in a welcoming and equitable class environment—and helps make it an attainable reality by providing clear guidance, helpful activities, and personal experiences.

—John Spinda, Assistant Professor, Clemson University

Students are no longer vessels to be filled with information; they want to know why. *Teaching From the Heart* helps faculty create socially just classrooms. From syllabi and office hours, to significant assignments and assessments, *Teaching From the Heart* will help faculty fill their courses with the WHY and as well as provide the HOW.

—Nick Burns, Associate Dean, Salt Lake Community College

TEACHING
FROM THE **HEART**
CRITICAL COMMUNICATION PEDAGOGY
IN THE COMMUNICATION CLASSROOM

**C. KYLE RUDICK, KATHRYN B. GOLSAN,
& KYLE CHEESEWRIGHT**

FIRST EDITION

cognella | ACADEMIC PUBLISHING

Bassim Hamadeh, CEO and Publisher
Kassie Graves, Director of Acquisitions and Sales
Jamie Giganti, Senior Managing Editor
Jess Estrella, Senior Graphic Designer
Jennifer McCarthy, Acquisitions Editor
Gem Rabanera, Project Editor
Alexa Lucido, Licensing Coordinator
Tracy Buyan, Associate Production Editor
Kevin Fontimayor, Interior Designer

Cover images: copyright © Depositphotos/artishokcs1.
copyright © Depositphotos/vectorguy.
copyright © Depositphotos/t30gallery.

Printed in the United States of America

ISBN:978-1-5165-1335-2 (pbk) / 978-1-5165-1336-9 (br)

This book is dedicated to John T. Warren
Our mentor
Thank you for believing in our work

All Royalties from this Textbook
will be Donated to the
Central States Communication Association's
John T. Warren Mentorship Award

CONTENTS

TABLE OF COMMUNICATION ACTIVITIES AND ORIENTATION CATEGORIES

RELATIONAL ORIENTATION

INSTITUTIONAL ORIENTATION

CULTURAL ORIENTATION

APPENDICES

FOREWORD

BY DEANNA L. FASSETT

"The academy is not paradise. But learning is a place where paradise can be created. The classroom, with all its limitations, remains a location of possibility. In that field of possibility we have the opportunity to labor for freedom, to demand of ourselves and our comrades, an openness of mind and heart that allows us to face reality even as we collectively imagine ways to move beyond boundaries, to transgress. This is education as the practice of freedom." (hooks, 1994, p. 207)

"Pedagogy as praxis is working with others to examine the possibilities implicit in constitutive theories of communication; it is to suggest that if we build our identities in contest and collusion with one another, if we create our pains and pleasures in communication, then perhaps we can interrupt those processes and shape them anew in meaningful ways." (Fassett & Warren, 2007, p. 51)

"All education serves as a strategic structuring of a student's relationship with 'reality.'" (Swartz, 1995, p. 131)

The John T. Warren you find referenced here and there and everywhere in this book felt very strongly that teaching and research are mutually informing. Though he and I would joke that I was a teacher who grudgingly engaged in research, and he was a researcher who grudgingly engaged in teaching, we were both wrong. I don't think either of us ever had a scholarly idea that wasn't in some way informed by our work in the classroom, and I don't think either of us ever taught a lesson that wasn't in some way informed by our own and others' research. In John's case, you could find notes about research and teaching equally represented in the margins of anything he was reading, just as surely as you would find comments about both in work he returned to colleagues and students. I especially loved how he'd write bits of lesson plans on cocktail napkins and business cards at conferences, tucking them into whatever he was reading, effectively capturing the inspiration and finding ways to nurture it in future readings. Teaching and research emerges from life, from conversations with others in and out of the academy, and helps make sensible all that can be confusing and painful about life, in all its facets.

The book you're reading evolved from and extends what is increasingly a rich heritage of critical cultural scholarship at the intersections of communication and instruction (Fassett & Rudick, 2016). It is here to help you think through your experiences in and of the classroom, as teachers, students, and, inevitably, researchers. Irrespective of whether you choose to put your insights into print, the classroom becomes a meaningful and tangible location for better understanding and practicing communication. As you already well know, education is not a "paradise," at least not in the traditional sense, but it is, as hooks (1994) so powerfully argues, "a location of possibility" (p. 207). It is in our interactions with others—whether students, educators, administrators, industry or other community members—that we can build a world that challenges us to grow and learn, from ourselves and each other. Further, it is in our substantive interactions with others that we can and must learn from the material experiences of people our society marginalizes, so that any of us and all of us can and must participate in the process of knowledge construction.

We live in a present where the work of teaching is vaunted, but neglected. A number of pressures, from the economic to the cultural, exist to shape teaching into communiques and teachers into presumably impartial conduits of established Truth. This book is a practical tool to resist these trends. This book introduces you to the history, the vocabulary, and the skillset you can use to work toward teaching and learning as a humanizing act, one that recognizes and values the life experiences of both teachers and learners, as well as the contingent and always political nature of truths. Teaching is a critical enterprise, and agreeing to teach is a significant responsibility.

That said, you need no specialized experience or prior knowledge to understand this book or engage in the processes the authors advocate. All you need is curiosity and a willingness to explore thorny and complex issues and experiences that most often simply do not have a single uncomplicated solution. This book marks a departure from other, seemingly acontextual or apolitical approaches to classroom instruction. Instead of sharing teaching tips or great ideas for teaching students, the authors remind us that "how to" questions—and especially "how to teach" questions—are always already situated in overlapping vectors of culture, ideology, and power.

This book will help you build and refine a vocabulary for reflexive analysis of what happens in classrooms. In some ways this will help you develop your thoughts about and experiences of the classroom for a more public—perhaps print—audience. But, perhaps more to the point, it is the classroom where you can and will change others, and others can and will change you. As Sprague (1993) notes, "For the majority of communication studies scholars pedagogy is our praxis. While we may write about organizations, the media, or politics, it is in our classrooms that we ourselves wield power and manipulate symbols with real consequences on other human lives" (p. 106). Rather than encountering the classroom as a chaotic and confusing place, you can use the concepts and theories the authors reference here to make meaning with the learners in your classrooms. You will learn alongside your students to "locate and name the taken-for-granted in pedagogical contexts, to decenter normative readings of a given phenomenon, experience or idea" (Fassett & Warren, 2007, p. 51). Though our own most deeply held assumptions about teaching and learning can make it difficult for us to understand education as persuasion, the authors here will model a compassionate self-inquiry that will help you learn and grow such that you can grow meaningfully into the role of someone who nurtures and motivates both others and yourself to question and engage the world inside and outside the classroom in collaborative and sustainable ways.

John T. Warren believed strongly that the college classroom could be a powerful site of change and justice. Not every moment or even every day can live up to that expectation, but the aspiration alone is important. It reminds us that teaching and learning—well, meaningfully, contextually—is possible ... and beautiful ... and confusing ... and lasting. I know he would have loved to know of your own struggles and successes with being fully present in the classroom, and I would, too. Communication (in and out of the classroom) creates—what will you, will we all, build?

REFERENCES

Fassett, D. L., & Rudick, C. K. (2016). Critical communication pedagogy. In P. L. Witt (Ed.), *Handbooks of communication science: Communication and learning* (vol. 16, pp. 573–598). Berlin, Germany: DeGruyter Mouton.
Fassett, D. L., & Warren, J. T. (2007). *Critical communication pedagogy*. Thousand Oaks, CA: Sage Publications.
hooks, b. (1994). *Teaching to transgress: Education as the practice of freedom*. New York, NY: Routledge.

Sprague, J. (1993). Retrieving the research agenda for communication education: Asking the pedagogical questions that are "embarrassments to theory." *Communication Education*, 42(2), 106–122. doi: 10.1080/03634529309378919

Swartz, O. (1995). Interdisciplinary and pedagogical implications of rhetorical theory. *Communication Studies*, 46(1-2), 130–139. doi: 10.1080/10510979509368444

PROLOGUE

HOW THIS BOOK GOT STARTED:
A SIX-YEAR JOURNEY

KYLE R.: This book got started in the fall of 2010, in John T. Warren's Critical Communication Pedagogy seminar at Southern Illinois University Carbondale. John had asked the class to read the *Critical Communication Pedagogy* book Deanna Fassett and he wrote and—and this was so typically John—he told the class, "I don't want you to think you have to be nice about the book because I'm in the room. I want you to tell me how we could make it better." As the class continued to discuss, we all warmed up to the idea of extending upon the work that John and Deanna started. And, as a class, we started talking about how to make critical communication pedagogy more explicit in the advice it offered new and continuing instructors.

KYLE C.: Yeah, and, to be fair, that critique is a pretty common theme in a lot of writing on critical forms of pedagogy. Translating the insights of critique into everyday practice is the hardest part for a lot of folks. And John always felt that tension keenly. He would say, "If I'm overly prescriptive about how to do critical communication pedagogy then I am deskilling teachers. I'm not letting them use their creative capacities. I am trading one set of technical skills of teaching for another. But, when I don't offer that advice, then people think it's all just high theory nonsense." It's so tough to know the right space to write from.

KYLE R.: Yeah, John recognized that young teachers, particularly those that have little formal training in any type of instructional philosophy, wanted guidance on things like classroom management or how to put a good syllabus together. One night, after class, a few students from the class got together to talk about writing a book that would help teachers address pragmatic concerns, but in a humane or humanizing way. So, we wrote a book proposal for the final paper in John's class. I've read our initial work (laughing) and it was pretty bad. But, John believed in us and told us to keep thinking and writing on it. And, then, unfortunately, he passed away that next spring. We promised ourselves that this idea—this idea that John believed in even though we were too young and green to properly handle it—would get published. It took six years of writing, rewriting, finding publishers, losing publishers, and finding new publishers. We were helped by amazing people, such as Kathy Hytten, Deanna Fassett, Sandy Pensoneau-Conway, and Keith Nainby. And now, this book, our labor of love to John and his belief in us, is finished.

KATHRYN But, our work as critical communication pedagogues is never really finished, is it? It's always in the process of becoming, of realizing something new, exciting, and fantastic.

PHILOSOPHY OF THE BOOK

KATHRYN: You all are talking about these pragmatic concerns in the classroom and critical communication pedagogy, but some people might not know what you're talking about. Like, what about instructors who receive no training at all? What would you do in that instance?

KYLE C.: I would have collapsed (laughing). It would be terrifying. I wasn't that much older than most of my students. In fact, many of my students were older than me. Walking into the classroom for the first time was one of the scariest things I've ever done.

KATHRYN: Do you remember the very first time you walked into your classroom to teach?

KYLE C.: (laughing) No, the whole first semester was a haze of panic and terror.

KATHRYN: (laughs) I was the same way! But, as I got more comfortable with my identity as a teacher, I began thinking about how to connect to peoples' experiences.

KYLE R.: You try to put on a good face, you know? You try to "act like a teacher," whatever that means. You mimic the good teachers you've had up until it's your turn to teach. Or, you try to avoid being like the really bad teachers you've studied under. And, that's helpful, but I would have liked someone to help me build up a mental framework for the things I have encountered as a teacher before having them dropped in my lap.

KATHRYN: Yeah, I think you have to get to a place where you feel comfortable with being uncomfortable.

KYLE C.: Yeah, because there's no way to be prepared for all of those things. The first time a student told me they were HIV positive I was certainly not prepared for that. Or, when I had other students talk to me about addictions they were struggling with or depression—there's just not a handbook. I don't think there can be a handbook that would work because your ability to respond is based on the relationship you have with those students.

KATHRYN: How did you figure out your own teaching philosophy? What kind of advice did you get when you started teaching?

KYLE C.: Well, I started out with teacher training that was much more about how to plan classes around and secure high learning outcomes, with some type of final assessment to measure my success. But, I never felt that I was getting down to the beauty of the classroom, so I started trying to do a lot of reading about social justice alongside that work.

KYLE R.: Yeah, I feel the same way. So much of traditional instruction really assumes that the classroom is a vacuum—you know, it's just about getting students to fulfill the goals or objectives that a teacher thinks are important as a sign that students are learning. I think that it's important to have that sort of intentionality, you know, always asking yourself, "Why am I assigning this paper or giving this lecture? What do I hope to accomplish?" But, that didn't help me answer the questions about all the things that are going on outside of the classroom that influence learning; things like racism, sexism, or rampant income inequality. The issues that institutions of higher education, and I as a teacher, both reflect and produce.

WHO WE ARE: IDENTITY IN PROCESS

KYLE C.: I'm always a little confused, you know. I'm concerned because how I identify is changing all of the time and constantly becoming something different. In terms of my generic positionality statement, I usually roll with Kyle Cheesewright—a White, temporarily able-bodied, male and masculine, gay-genderqueer academic of fairly fluid class status. I actually developed that positionality statement in one of John's classes. I try to account for how others perceive me as well as how I perceive myself, which challenges me to identify the tensions within the process of identity making. My identity is always hard to talk about explicitly in the classroom. I was taught, as a new teacher, that I should absolutely never "come out" in the classroom because it will lower my teacher evaluation scores.

KYLE R.: I definitely don't experience the class the same way you do because I don't think my body invites questions of credibility. I identify as White, male, and middle class, visibly able-bodied and heterosexual. Whenever people look at me there is a sort of credibility that a person has for someone like me because I present in so many traditionally privileged categories.

KATHRYN: I get questioned about my credibility a lot. I'm a White female. I'm short with dyed red hair. And, even though my education helps me perform middle class, I grew up in poverty and sometimes it's really hard to know how to interact, how to perform like a good, middle-class professional. I feel, on a daily basis, the differences when interacting with higher- and middle-class people—it makes me feel like an imposter, like I don't belong in higher education.

KYLE C.: The focus on positionality plays out most clearly in the ways that I like to incorporate and try to refer to stories as ways to speak to identities that may seem invisible or play out in different ways. I also try to talk to students about some of the struggles that I've had with identities. Like, I associate with genderqueer, but I'm terrified to perform that in a classroom. I think that locating your positionality is an important place to start exploring questions of privilege and power.

KATHRYN: Sometimes I don't want to talk about my identity either. Especially my poverty background, because that is one of the hardest things for people to embrace as a positive in higher education, like it's such a taboo to talk about social class. But, I keep doing it because students visit me after class, in my office, or over email, saying, "I'm so glad that you said that because I want to share my struggles too."

KYLE R.: The way that I see my positionalities operating for me is inhabiting this sort of dual status. I try to recognize the power that I wield in the classroom, or society, because of the body that I inhabit and the historic moment in which I live. On one hand, how can I use my body, my credibility, to appropriately amplify the voices of people who are marginalized? How can I speak with them in ways that ensure their concerns are listened to in society? On the other hand, when is it my role to shut up, step back, or listen? How can I work *for* marginalized people and not about or without them?

KATHRYN: I think it's really important for a new instructors and graduate student-teachers, especially those who identify more with privileged positions, to realize and take to heart that their work, any work, is contextual, relational, and historical. That's why it's so complicated, right? There are no easy answers.

FAILURE AND HOPE: LEARNING FROM JOHN

KYLE R.: I hope that people who read this book really understand teaching as relationship building. And, not just in the sort of empty, shiny red apple and ruler, "Oh I love my students" sort of soundbite relationship, but as a way to deeply invest in students. At the same time, how students respond to teachers, how teachers respond to them—well, on some level there's no how-to manual for that work.

KYLE C.: I think that's a really nice segue for talking about John as a mentor. For me, he was very much about trying to get folks to recognize that you're not always going to have the right answer. And, that's okay; it's going to be hard. There will be days when you'll be exhausted, but you can cut yourself some slack as long as you continue to return to asking the sort of questions that push us to work for and with our students to realize a better world.

KYLE R.: I think what you just said was so incredibly important. When you mess up or think you've failed, you have to commit to having conversations with your students and peers, to learn and continue to chafe at your limits and strive to be better for other people. I think that's one thing I always appreciated about John. He was so prolific, so smart, so humble, and so vulnerable. John was so invested in seeing other people succeed. So much of his published work is co-authored because he genuinely enjoyed investing in other people, and letting them invest in him, to create better ideas.

KATHRYN: (laughs) You know he would be embarrassed that you said that about him. He would never think that he was all of those things.

KYLE C.: (laughs) Yeah, but let's be honest, as a second-year professor his publication record was probably better than all three of ours put together. But, you would have never known that when you were hanging out with him.

KATHRYN: I love the way that Deanna talks about him, how he was constantly worried and anxious because people knew him as the "Whiteness guy." He didn't like the spotlight. He just wanted more for the people around him, and never thought he was doing enough.

KYLE R.: John taught me that there is not a magic bullet to critical communication pedagogy, no one way to do it "right." He also taught me that when I'm teaching, it is okay to admit failure or work through a process in front of my students. I always felt so much pressure to be perfect, but perfection is just a myth and chasing it will make you either unhappy because you can't find it or a narcissist because you think you have.

KATHRYN: I always think, if I ever think that teaching is easy, it's because I'm just going through the motions at that point. If it's too easy, I should really stop myself and examine what I'm doing, because teaching should never be easy.

KYLE R.: I think you're absolutely right. Teaching for social justice is hard, it requires courage, commitment, and humility. And, if you stop feeling uncomfortable then you need to ask yourself, "Am I really doing social justice work anymore?" Because if you think teaching for social justice is easy, it's probably because you're avoiding the hard work that comes with listening to and investing in others.

KATHRYN: You have to be mindful. And that's a constant struggle.

WHAT WE HOPE THIS BOOK DOES

KATHRYN: I hope people know that what we have done here, how we think about critical communication pedagogy, is just a little sliver of all the work that is out there on social justice. Each article, book, or chapter is a labor of love, calling us to humanize ourselves and each other.

KYLE R.: You're right. Each one of those projects consists of countless unseen hours of late-night conversations, reading other peoples' work, thinking about these things, talking more, and going through draft after draft. I'm especially proud that our book has a place for the teaching activities. Graduate students, early career professors, and established scholars all contributed to the section, and I am so happy that there are so many voices that get a chance to be heard. And, I think that it's important that we recognize all of their hard work, and how they help this book to be better than it would have been without their voices.

KYLE C.: I feel like that's the ethic we have tried to have in our writing—that what we put on the page isn't just words for other people to read. Our writing is a promise to live up to our espoused ideals, calling us to be better teachers, researchers, and activists for social justice.

KATHRYN: And this book isn't a product; it's not complete or finished. It opens up avenues for conversations about social justice in education. We hope each page encourages readers to be better than us. Hopefully, they will become mentors like John, who will support students as they articulate how to make this book, this movement, this world, better.

SOCIAL JUSTICE, CRITICAL COMMUNICATION PEDAGOGY, AND THE COMMUNICATION CLASSROOM

CRITICAL COMMUNICATION PEDAGOGY IS SOCIAL JUSTICE, AS DEFINED, EXPLORED, AND IMPLEMENTED WITHIN A COMMUNITY OF CARING AND GENEROUS BELIEVERS IN FREEDOM, AND JUSTICE, AND LOVE—FOR ALL, ALL THE TIME.

FASSETT AND WARREN (2007, P. 128)

IN THE COMMUNICATION STUDIES DEPARTMENT OF SOUTHERN ILLINOIS UNIVERSITY, GRADUATE STUDENTS OFTEN SAID: "JOHN T. WARREN MOVES LIKE A SPACESHIP." Through the construction of a joking collegiality, students recognized that John, or JTW as he was often called, had a frenetic energy, a driving force to help discover things that were hard to imagine before one set out on their journey. As an instructor and a mentor, JTW had a powerful and obvious influence on each of the authors of this book, such that it is hard for us to imagine a different way of living.

Before his untimely passing in 2011, John worked, talked, laughed, and collaborated with each of us. Although we knew him for only a short length of time, each of us continues to work toward his goal of transforming the communication discipline to embrace social justice through critical communication pedagogy (Fassett & Warren, 2007). We fell in love with his work, but more than that we fell in love with him: his spirit, his intelligence, his love for shoes. We have written this book with the hope of continuing his legacy as a communication scholar who was deeply invested in continuing conversations about oppression and privilege through the communication class. This book is how we try to honor him—by working to realize his dream of critical communication pedagogy and social justice scholarship becoming widely recognized approaches to communication instruction. We hope that you too are interested in pursuing his dream.

We want to share with you our love for working with students to create lasting and meaningful relationships across and through our differences. We recognize that (in many departments) course textbooks are chosen at the departmental level with little or no input by a single instructor. This trend is particularly true in programs that rely heavily upon adjunct and graduate-student instructors to oversee communication courses. However, whether you currently use a textbook that utilizes a critical perspective, such as *Communication: A Critical/Cultural Introduction* (Warren & Fassett, 2014), *Empowering Public Speaking* (Fassett & Nainby, forthcoming), or some other text(s), we hope that you are committed to expanding conversations about the importance of fostering social justice within and through your classes.

Your choice to read this book signals that you, like us, want to do the hard work that comes with being a social justice instructor. In this text, we will discuss social justice theory, critical communication pedagogy, and classroom practices. Throughout the course of this text, we will try not to present our advice as "Truth," rather, we strive towards Freire's (2006) notion of *praxis*; that is, the notion that our teaching practices should inform our educational theories, and vice versa. This ethic encourages us to resist one-size-fits-all answers, focusing instead on teaching and learning as situated, contextual, and relational (Rudick & Golsan, 2014; Sprague, 1992). We are reminded of Dannels' (2014) assertion that teaching is not just hard work, it is heart work. In other words, teaching is about content, but (more than that) what we teach is made meaningful through collaboration with and among students.

In this chapter, we will theoretically frame this book within social justice theory and critical communication pedagogy. We want to assure you that we do not believe in academic jargon for the sake of jargon, but, as John loved to remind us (usually when we complained after reading a particularly long-winded journal article), "NASA scientists don't send people up to the moon by calling the parts of a rocket doo-hickeys and thingamabobs. Sophisticated and precise operations call for sophisticated and precise language." We believe that teaching is a sophisticated and precise operation. Learning and practicing a common set of language tools about communication and instruction recognizes the hard intellectual and emotional labor of teaching, and sets the stage for dialogues among social justice–minded instructors about the best practices for critical communication pedagogical work.

WHAT IS SOCIAL JUSTICE?

During our own time in grad school, we spent many long evenings in seminars, living rooms, and backyards discussing and debating what it means to engage in "social justice" advocacy. Although the term *social justice* is regularly used by activists and scholars, there are wide disagreements as to what it means. For the purposes of this book, we will draw upon the definition given by Bell (2007), because she defines social justice as both a process and a goal. As a process, social justice utilizes participatory and democratic methods in order to transform unequal power relations. As a goal, social justice "includes a vision of society in which the distribution of resources is *equitable* and all members are physically and psychologically secure" (p. 1). When students and instructors engage in dialogue, community involvement, and reflexive thinking, we believe they can then promote social justice within and beyond the classroom; though, like all things worth investigating,

> **social justice**
> the process and goal by which people work together to transform unequal power relations to realize a world where all people feel emotionally, physically, and economically secure to realize their full capabilities
>
> **equitable**
> equity means that each person receives support relative to their needs. Often contrasted with equality, which means each person receives the same level of support regardless of their specific needs.

we recognize our belief is open to contestation. Although social justice education is not easy, we argue that a social justice framework offers the best hope for people to cultivate meaningful, authentic, and equitable relationships with one another.

Although some political pundits and scholars believe that society is largely equal, and that one's successes and failures are based primarily on individual work ethic, the assumption that we bring to this book is that there remain deeply embedded systems of oppression and privilege within contemporary society. This is an assumption that we share with a large number of scholars, based on the work of researchers who argue that oppressive systems such as *racism, sexism, genderism, dis/ableism,* and *classism* are deeply embedded within education (see Adams, Bell, & Griffin, 2007). As long as these systems of inequity persist, we believe that it is our moral obligation as critical educators and scholars to teach through and about social justice as a way to resist and transform oppressive systems.

> **racism**
> beliefs, norms, and attitudes, operating at all levels of society and with(out) conscious intent, that reinforce the subjugation of people color and perpetuate White supremacy

sexism
beliefs, norms, and attitudes, operating at all levels of society and with(out) conscious intent, that reinforce the subjugation of women and perpetuate patriarchy

genderism
beliefs, norms, and attitudes, operating at all levels of society and with(out) conscious intent, that reinforce the subjugation of gender non-conforming people and perpetuate cisgender (i.e., people who identify with their assigned gender identity) normalcy

dis/ableism
ableism refers to beliefs, norms, and attitudes that reinforce the perceived normalcy of particular psychological, emotional, or physical abilities, whereas disableism refers to the oppression of people with perceived impairments. Dis/ableism is meant to capture both of these dynamics, which operates at all levels of society and with(out) conscious intent, reinforcing the subjugation of disabled people and perpetuating able-bodiedness (i.e., the notion that certain bodies are normal).

Conversation concerning oppression and privilege are at the heart of social justice theory. We utilize Hardiman, Jackson, and Griffin's (2007) definition of *oppression*, which defines it as "a system that maintains advantage and disadvantage based on social group memberships and operates, intentionally and unintentionally, on individual, institutional, and cultural levels" (p. 58). Important to their definition is the notion that oppression refers to more than just individual experiences. For example, Kathryn Golsan and Kyle Rudick are diagnosed with attention deficit disorder (ADD) and sometimes utilize prescription medicine to help them focus on their work (including writing this book!). However, they do not feel that being diagnosed ADD defines them as disabled. Rather, it is the interconnection among the individual (e.g., being called stupid), institutional (e.g., lack of ADD-sensitive testing for the ACT or SAT), and cultural (e.g., being thought of as abnormal compared to so-called able-bodied individuals) that constitutes their dis/ableism. Therefore, it may be more accurate to say that *people are disabled by society*, than to say that a *person is disabled* (Golsan & Rudick, 2015).

The corollary to oppression is privilege. Drawing upon Hardiman et al. (2007), we choose to define *privilege* as the unearned access to resources (whether social or material) that some individuals receive due to their perceived membership in a social group. Privilege can prompt different responses to oppression and oppressive systems. Returning to our example about dis/ableism and ADD, a person's privilege may engender different reactions to dis/ability, such as ignorance (e.g., "I never thought we needed multiple ways to teach students"), pity (e.g., "Oh! Those poor people just can't think like normal people!"), dismissal (e.g., "Medical companies invented ADD just to make money. It really doesn't exist."), or anger (e.g., "People with ADD are bad students who don't want to study hard like me!"). Privilege harms our ability to communicate across and about our differences toward social justice goals. Recognizing the existence of privilege can be difficult, but through examining and reflectively engaging with systems of privilege, social justice education can help us discover ways to transform privilege into action for equity, helping to avoid these common types of unreflective responses to structural discrimination.

Although many well-meaning educators desire to make their classrooms *inclusive* spaces, it is easy to rely upon outdated notions of multiculturalism or diversity. Our own observations have resulted in our belief that diversity initiatives are often predicated upon the notion that cultural differences should be tolerated rather than explored as meaningful sites of discovery and growth (Kanpol, 1999). As such, they have the unfortunate tendency to relativize power (e.g., we're all different, so we're all the same), tokenize (e.g., acting as if one student of color can speak for all people of her/his race), or promote a sense of cultural tourism (e.g., eating sushi to appear "cultured"). Unfortunately, diversity programs do not often offer viable alternatives to dominant forms of knowledge; instead, these approaches exoticize oppressed people's knowledges. As Darder (1991) explains:

> classism
> beliefs, norms, and attitudes, operating at all levels of society and with(out) conscious intent, that reinforce hierarchies of people based factors, such as educational attainment, income, and ownership of property. Classism is a necessary condition to a capitalist society.

> oppression
> a system that maintains hierarchical relationships based on perceived group membership

> privilege
> unearned access to resources (whether social or material) that some individuals receive due to their perceived membership in a social group

> Multicultural materials and activities do not, in and of themselves, ensure that a culturally democratic process is at work ... and many situations exist in which students are presented with games, food, stories, language, music, and other cultural forms in such a way as to strip these expressions of intent by reducing them to mere objects disembodied from their cultural meaning. (p. 113)

Many diversity efforts are predicated upon the notion that the mere presence of diverse bodies (e.g., having an equal representation of people of different races) is enough to ensure that oppression is adequately challenged. We argue that diversity initiatives within higher education are insufficient to displace oppressive practices within and beyond the classroom. We believe that inclusive classrooms can only be realized when we explicitly and intentionally attend to the dynamics of oppression and privilege through social justice (Rudick & Golsan, 2016). The seeming ubiquity of these problematic approaches to social justice education was often the topic of our conversations during graduate school, and will remain a topic of conversation for us in the future. But through these discussions, and the guidance of JTW, one way that we have found to work through these conflicts and toward social justice is the use of critical communication pedagogy.

> **inclusive**
> an environment, culture, or space that meaningfully incorporates and affirms all types of people

WHAT DOES SOCIAL JUSTICE HAVE TO DO WITH TEACHING COMMUNICATION?

As we have taught through and about social justice we have often been interrogated about why we want to discuss privilege and oppression in our communication classrooms. Our experiences have lead us to believe that these responses are based upon the notion that classroom content should be neutral or objective, and that social justice theories are unnecessary add-ons (at best), or attempts to inject liberal bias into the class (at worst; Applebaum, 2009). Instructors who identify within oppressed groups (e.g., people of color, dis/abled people, women, or trans folk) are often disproportionately targeted with these questions. For example, Patton (2004), who identifies as a female of color, documented times when her White students asked her to stop talking about race and gender in her communication class, and only teach about "real" issues. Overall, these responses seek to reinforce the ways students, instructors, and administrators have (un)consciously thought about education—as a system of cultural practice that reflects the cultural knowledges, histories, or desires of privileged groups.

Within the past 20 years, communication scholars have become increasingly sensitive to conversations concerning social justice and communication courses (e.g., Hendrix, Mazer, and Hess, 2016, editors of a special issue of *Communication Education* on diversity). Critical communication pedagogy (CCP) has emerged as an important theoretical contribution to these discussions. CCP draws upon *critical pedagogy* (e.g., Freire, 2006) and *postmodern theory* (e.g., Butler, 1991) to focus on how everyday acts of communication, both within and beyond the classroom, function to "teach" individuals to (not) see privilege and oppression in the world. Importantly, CCP seeks to sensitize students and instructors to the ways that traditional "neutral" instruction curtails their creative capacity to learn about and transform their everyday communicative practices. Overall, a CCP perspective encourages instructors understand that there is no such thing as a neutral or objective education, but rather ways of teaching that either encourage or discourage the ability to perceive, challenge, and transform systems of oppression and privilege.

Recently, one of us was teaching a class in which we were examining the role of *race-neutral policies* in dealing with racism, when a student in the classroom raised their hand. This student proceeded to read a section of another class's textbook that dismissed social justice strategies of engagement (e.g., affirming difference). The student's textbook proposed that race-neutral policies were the only method to effectively combat racism, and that the social justice–oriented reading that we had done for class was "biased." As we discussed these two texts in our classroom, we noticed that the student's text presented itself as a "neutral, objective" source, but did not engage with any of the complex scholarship critiquing race-neutral policies that existed in our class reading for the day. Through examining how a seemingly "neutral and objective" source ignored the large amount of research that challenged its perspective, we were able to discuss how the presentation of information as "neutral and objective" might result in stifling creative challenges to a text, and allow power to continue to operate with as little challenge to systems of privilege and oppression as possible.

critical pedagogy
a social, political, and intellectual movement that seeks to identify and challenge the ways that institutions of education tacitly or overtly support dominant interests

postmodern
literally "after modernism," the postmodern movement is characterized by a rejection of narratives, theories, or philosophies that attempt to offer a singular explanation or Truth (with a capital T)

race-neutral policies
often called "colorblind" policies in literature (a phrase we have recently dropped due to its dis/ableist tones), race-neutral policies refer to rules, laws, or norms that purportedly ignore racial group membership and treat everyone as human

The insights of critical communication pedagogy are therefore of great importance to communication course instructors. We believe that learning and teaching communication theories, ethics, concepts, or public speaking skills that are divorced from a concern with social justice leaves systems of oppression and privilege in place. As Schaull (2006) so succinctly puts it,

> Education either functions as an instrument that is used to facilitate the integration of the younger generation into the logic of the present system and bring about conformity to it, *or* it becomes "the practice of freedom," the means by which men and women deal critically and creatively with reality and discover how to participate in the transformation of their world. (p. 34)

Teaching public speaking as a set of skills that is disconnected from history, context, and power, or communication theory as a hodgepodge of key terms with no relation to students' lived experiences, functions to disempower them as creative, transformative change agents. Our argument in this book is that communication course instructors have a duty to their students to teach skills and theories that empower students to challenge and change oppression and privilege in their lives. We hope that this book can serve as an important step for you as you start on or continue your journey as a social justice–minded instructor.

TEXTBOOK'S PURPOSE AND OUTLINE

The primary focus of this book is to help new and continuing instructors understand how to teach about and through critical communication pedagogy in the communication course. Although we frame our textbook using theoretical tools from communication and education studies, we try to focus on the pragmatic questions of instruction (e.g., syllabus construction). Where we depart from most textbooks that deal with pragmatic issues is our focus on how to answer these questions with practices grounded in social justice. To that end, we begin our chapters with a narrative and a social justice concept to frame our discussion. We then visit a host of concerns and address each through the concept we have introduced. Finally, we provide questions at the end of each chapter to give you a journal prompt. We encourage you to keep a journal about your classroom teaching as you practice the concepts that you have learned about in this text in order to become an intentional, self-reflective instructor. Below contains an outline of the next seven chapters of this book, so you know what to expect as you work your way through this text.

In Chapter Two, "Critical Frames for Communication Pedagogy," we outline the history of critical communication pedagogy, describe its 10 commitments, and apply those concepts to the introductory communication course. In doing so, we offer a discipline-specific language for talking about social justice concepts. Importantly, we include ongoing research utilizing critical communication pedagogy in the hope that you will engage in the scholarly conversations about social justice education emerging in our discipline.

In Chapter Three, "Positioning/Orienting Toward the Communication Classroom," we talk about how higher education's rules and norms create a culture of power (Delpit, 1988). Because many instructors have advanced degrees and/or have spent many years in academia, it is sometimes difficult for us to recognize that what we think of as normal or common sense actually reflects our own biases. Furthermore, when we (un)intentionally overvalue the knowledges of dominant people, we can alienate students from their ability to be transformative change agents. These concerns are particularly salient when an instructor identifies with dominant cultural positions (e.g., White, heterosexual, and/or male). As such, we encourage instructors to become intentional in their efforts to demystify the culture of power and their culpability in its maintenance. We use this framework to talk about issues that arise in the first few weeks of the semester (or even before it begins!), such as syllabus construction, reading lists, and dress codes.

In Chapter Four, "Assessment and Power in the Communication Classroom," we frame our discussion in the concept of the hidden curriculum (Giroux & Penna, 1983). As Gatto (2006) argues, although there are certainly explicit lessons taught in each class (e.g., how to give a speech), every institution of education also (un)intentionally teaches students to defer to authority, maintain silence, and discipline their bodies. We believe that when instructors are not intentional and reflexive, they run the risk of passing oppressive hidden lessons on to students. Assessment is often the way that the lessons of hidden curriculum are enforced. We argue that students should be encouraged to view classroom assignments as opportunities to take risks and explore their creative capacities, rather than as an imposition of facts, dates, and terms. Central to this mission is the notion that assessment should function as a conversation starter rather than closer. Drawing upon this perspective, we offer public speeches, essays, and portfolios as common assessment tools that can be used toward social justice goals.

In Chapter Five, "Mentoring as an Act of Love in the Communication Classroom," we draw upon the work of bell hooks (1994) and Freire (2006) to discuss love in the classroom. We argue that the idea of loving our students is still viewed with suspicion in the academy. In the quest to be viewed as knowledge-able content experts, instructors sometimes speak from the head when we should speak from the heart. By working toward social justice with an ethic of love, we can practice communication with others that seeks to respect, affirm, and explore our cultural differences. By recognizing and cultivating loving relationships with students, instructors can model how to have sensitive and sensitizing contact with others. We focus on attendance, classroom participation, and office hours as activities that are often viewed with disdain or contempt, but that we believe can be crucial sites to begin fostering relationships between and among students and instructors.

In Chapter Six, "Critical Dialogue and Pitfalls in the Communication Classroom," we argue that the communication course can and should be a site for social justice activism. We utilize the concept of critical dialogue (Freire, 2006) as a type of intentional communicative act that challenges oppressive systems within and beyond the classroom. Central to this understanding of dialogue is the notion that the instructors and students should work toward collaboratively exploring the problems that face society and jointly articulating ways to transform those situations. Critical dialogue, in this sense, focuses our attention on how talking about our problems can encourage us to think, act, and communicate in ways that challenge and change oppressive systems. We outline pitfalls to critical dialogue in the communication classroom through the concepts of hegemonic civility, resistance, activism, and sermonizing.

In Chapter Seven, "Chafing at Our Limits in the Communication Classroom," we utilize the term reflexivity (Freire, 2006) to help remind us of our obligation to constantly strive for a better understanding of ourselves in relation to our students and our advocacy. The term reflexivity asks us to continually ask more from ourselves, to chafe at the idea that who we are in this moment is the best possible version of ourselves. Reflexivity means working with others to situate our work within a coalition of voices that articulate a vision of the world as a place with less suffering. One way that we can work toward reflexive practices is to create and implement opportunities for students and instructors to intervene into the daily cycle of business as usual in the classroom in order to imagine new ways of interacting. We focus on institutional evaluations, self-created evaluations, and peer evaluations.

In Chapter Eight, "Social Justice Classroom Activities for the Communication Classroom," we have solicited the work of graduate-student instructors, beginning instructors, and long-term faculty to create a collection of social justice–oriented teaching activities. Drawing upon Pineau's (2004) work in critical performative pedagogy, we think that classroom activities are more than just a chance to be the fun instructor; they can be sites of self-discovery, creativity, and growth. These activities are not prescriptions for good teaching; rather, good teaching is a grounded in our relationships with students and enacted through dialogue. Activities provide the space by which students and instructors can come to challenge each other and, through that difference, grow together (Freire, 2006).

CONCLUSION

As we draw this chapter to a close, we wish to admit that our desire to write this book does not come from a belief that we are expert instructors. We do not think that we have all the answers, nor can we claim that we can address every concern. Teaching is a messy, complicated, and situated practice that will be shaped by your failures just as much as your successes. During one of our early days teaching in the Southern Illinois University Communication Department, Kyle C. accidentally slept through an alarm. Teaching at 8:00 a.m., this oversight meant that he missed his class—on the day he was to administer his midterm. As he walked into the Communication Building, clearly upset, he happened to wander past JTW. John gave him single look, up and down, and said, "I don't know what happened, but you look upset. If you want to come talk about it, you can. But remember, you have to be kind to yourself."

As you rush from classroom to classroom over the next few years, there will be days that you will fail to be the person you want to be in the classroom—times when you come home only to fall on your couch and weep in frustration and shame. There will be days that your students fail to be the people you wish them to be in the classroom—times when they say and do things that crush your spirit. There is no formula for teaching from the heart. But, if we wish to learn how to make a difference, then we must work together to transform ourselves and our classrooms. We, students and instructors, deserve no less than a world where we are free to live a life of equality, harmony, and love. And, we hope you will continue the hard work of teaching until this dream can be realized. In the meantime, we hope that you remember to be kind to yourself.

Journal/Discussion Questions

1. What are ways that you see privilege/oppression manifest in your life or society? How can those experiences help guide your teaching?
2. What role can you, as a communication studies scholar, play in promoting social justice in education and society?
3. If objectivity or neutrality are impossible, then does that mean that there is no such things as "information" or "facts"? How can you claim to be a content expert or someone who should be listened to as an instructor while believing that objective facts do not exist?

CRITICAL FRAMES FOR COMMUNICATION PEDAGOGY

CRITICAL COMMUNICATION PEDAGOGY, AS BOTH A FIELD OF STUDY AND A PEDAGOGICAL PRACTICE, IS SOMEWHERE IN THE NEXUS OF THE OVERLAPPING AREAS OF INTEREST.

FASSETT AND WARREN (2007, P. 38)

WE (KATHRYN AND KYLE R.) WALK INTO THE ROOM (HUSHED AND EMBARRASSED BECAUSE WE'RE LATE) TO WATCH JOHN WARREN PRESENT AT THE CENTRAL STATES COMMUNICATION ASSOCIATION. The panel is a spotlight honoring his work, a remarkable event given his youth in the field, but completely appropriate given the quantity and quality of his work. He sits in the middle of a long table, flanked on either side by friends, colleagues, and mentors, wearing a pink button-down shirt with the sleeves rolled up on both arms. We found out later that he has loved rocking that shirt at conferences ever since Dr. Scott Myers, an instructional communication scholar, called him "Ms. Pretty-in-Pink" in front of a room of scholars (much to John's blushing pleasure).

John is obviously uncomfortable with the attention. He fidgets in his seat, makes notes on a paper pad, and grimaces/smiles when someone compliments his research, giving almost every nonverbal indicator that he wishes he was anywhere else on the planet. But they don't stop; each, in turn, talks about how John's work influenced their own, his dedication to social justice, and their hope that critical communication pedagogy will spark a disciplinary movement toward critical approaches to pedagogy within the field. We sit in rapt attention, making notes, and whispering back and forth about a citation we want to track down or a concept that interests us.

After the panel is over, we want to talk with John, but there are too many people who want to shake his hand, ask a question, or compliment him. By the time we make it to the front of the room, he's somehow managed to disappear. We see Dr. Keith Berry, who we know from his work in relational communication, identity, and autoethnography, and ask him what happened to John. "Oh, you know John," Keith chuckles. "He took the first opportunity to get out of the room. All this attention makes him nervous." A bit disappointed, we leave to attend other conference panels and learn from members in our field.

Later that evening, we are in the conference hotel bar and we spy John sitting with his colleague Dr. Satoshi Toyosaki, who writes about autoethnography and intercultural communication. John's wearing his pink shirt, drinking red wine (a pinot noir, his favorite kind, we later learn), and talking with Satoshi, who also presented on the spotlight panel. We approach their table, introduce ourselves, and compliment both on their presentations. They ask us to sit with them and, excited, we do. We start to talk about John's work, but we realize after a few minutes that John has deftly changed the conversation from questions about his work to questions about ours. Minutes turn into hours and by the end of the evening we feel like we've told John everything—what we study, why we study it, and what we hope to accomplish in the field. "I think you'd be a great fit at SIU," John says as Satoshi nods. "Have you ever thought of applying there for your PhD?" Weak kneed and starry eyed—that was how we left our first conversation with John Warren.

***

communication education
the study of how to best teach communication skills, theories, and principles to students

instructional communication
the study of how teachers should (not) communicate with students to enhance learning, regardless of discipline or context

The study of communication as it occurs within educational contexts (e.g., higher education) has traditionally been the domain of study of *communication education* and *instructional communication* scholars. As Staton (1989) delineates,

Communication education ... one of the oldest fields of study of our discipline, is the study of the teaching of speech communication. ... The focus in the field is on the content, methods, strategies, evaluation, and materials for teaching speech communication.

... Instructional communication is defined typically as the study of the human communication process as it occurs in instructional contexts—across subject matter, grade levels, and types of settings. (p. 365)

In other words, communication education is teaching others how to teach the knowledge of the communication discipline (e.g., how to deliver a speech), whereas instructional communication focuses on the communicative behaviors between students and teachers, to find communication strategies that enhance learning outcomes. These two fields are characterized primarily by quantitative research designs (particularly post 1980), and have sought to articulate what constitutes effective pedagogy (whether within or beyond the communication discipline).

When we were master's students, we each went to programs that had a strong focus in instructional communication. West Virginia University, Kent State University, and California State University, Long Beach are home to some of the most prolific and respected instructional communication scholars in the discipline. Within those programs, we found people dedicated to promoting student learning, who spent their lives exploring the ways that instructors can engage in a host of communicative behaviors (e.g., self-disclosure, immediacy, and affinity-seeking strategies) to aid students. Although we respected (and still appreciate) their work, we struggled to find a home for the questions that drew us to the study of communication and sparked our love for pedagogy—questions about power, identity, context, and inequality in teaching and learning. It was during the final year of our programs that we each encountered Deanna L. Fassett and John Warren's text *Critical Communication Pedagogy.* As we read (and reread) the text, we realized that the chance to imagine and pursue answers to our questions would be found within this emerging tradition.

Critical communication pedagogy (CCP), "as a field of study and a pedagogical practice" (Fassett & Warren, 2007, p. 38), extends and (re)specifies the academic fields of communication education and instructional communication by drawing on various critical and postmodern traditions. In other words, CCP takes up the same areas of investigation as communication education and instructional communication, but has a radically different view of what constitutes "good" teaching. Whereas the traditional areas of the field focus primarily on what constitutes effective or efficient teaching practices, CCP asks, "Do teaching and learning perpetuate or challenge privilege and oppression?" CCP scholars are, of course, interested in effective teaching and learning, but only insofar as such practices are encompassed within the process and product of social justice education (see Chapter 1).

In this section, we outline the history and commitments of critical communication pedagogy. We encourage you to read Fassett and Warren's text, as well as other scholars' writings on the perspective (Allen, 2011; Fassett & Rudick, 2016; Warren, 2009). Doing so will offer you the chance to imagine and pursue answers to the questions that interest you about teaching and learning. One of John's favorite quotes, which adorned every one of his syllabi, was "To *live life* fully is to *live* it as if it were an *act of criticism*" (Marranca, 1985, p. 11). You may disagree with some of the ways we represent CCP or with some of the commitments of the perspective. Engaging a text on your terms, and exploring the ways it helps you make meaning within the classroom, is an important part of learning within a social justice perspective. And, if you ever want to talk about your understanding of social justice education, then email us or (better yet) meet us at a conference—we'll be happy to chat over a glass of pinot noir.

CRITICAL COMMUNICATION PEDAGOGY: 10 COMMITMENTS FOR SOCIAL JUSTICE EDUCATORS

Critical communication pedagogy owes a large intellectual debt to Jo Sprague who, in a series of essays in the 1990s and 2000s, argued that mainstream instructional communication and communication education scholars' emphasis on studying effective instruction ignored the social, cultural, and political dimensions of teaching and learning. For example, in asking "What is knowledge?" (1992, p. 11; see also Sprague, 1993, 1994, 2002), she challenged scholars to recognize that treating course content as a series of "facts" that must be memorized and recited disempowers students to develop their creative capacities as knowledge producers. She argued that by conflating classroom management with learning, traditional scholars neglected their ethical obligation to treat students as subjects, and their disciplinary responsibility to study the communicative negotiation of meaning-making in the classroom. The trajectory of her work called communication scholars to develop a communication-specific understanding of teaching and learning—a perspective that would be sensitive to power, language, and identity.

Many communication scholars sought to address her concerns through various perspectives, including critical pedagogy, feminist theory, and performance studies (see *Communication Education*, 2003, issues 3–4 for excellent examples). However, Fassett and Warren's book was the first text that sought to encapsulate the various strands of social justice education scholarship in communication studies and Sprague's work into a coherent whole. Their perspective is the product of dozens of scholars, decades of research, and countless conversations at conferences and in classrooms. We hope that you will add your voice to this important movement within the discipline, and help change the ways scholars in our field think, talk, and teach about and within the classroom.

Below we outline Fassett and Warren's (2007) 10 commitments of critical communication pedagogy to provide you with a framework for beginning your journey. As they caution in their text, these commitments are not meant to be a litmus test of how dedicated you are to social justice, nor are they an exhaustive list of precepts that one must slavishly adhere to in their teaching or research. Rather, they are conversation starters, concepts that you and others can use to begin your discussions about the nature of power, language, and identity in the communication classroom. Although Fassett and Warren address both teaching and research practices in their commitments (arguing that they are mutually informing), we focus primarily on how these commitments manifest in teaching.

COMMITMENT 1: IDENTITY IS CONSTITUTED IN COMMUNICATION

From *Men Are From Mars, Women Are From Venus* types of books in popular press, to the ways that media outlets portray the habits and dispositions of gay and straight men in shows such as *Modern Family*, many peoples' understanding of others is based on stereotypical views. This problem is especially true within media portrayals of students from poverty and students of color. Movies such as *Dangerous Minds*, *The Blind Side*, and *Waiting for Superman* give the impression that students from the margins need White, middle/upper class people to save them by teaching the socially inferior *Other* dominant cultural norms. In this view, identities, such as race, class, gender, or sexuality, are viewed as objective facts (e.g., female students talk/act/

Other
a term from postmodern philosophy, the Other (with a capital O) is the terrifying, amazing, or fantastic, often associated with cultures that one is not a part of, and often oppressed by a dominant culture

think differently than male students), and people are supposed to act as if these categories are objective and natural.

Critical communication pedagogy diverges sharply from this tradition by asserting that identities are socially constructed and performatively (re)constituted (see also Butler, 1990). In other words, identities are the product of societal habits, dispositions, or ways of talking that characterize an identity *and* the ways people take up, resist, defer, or subvert those norms. For example, in current Western civilizations, female and male are often the binary gender roles for people—a system that is (re)produced through medical terminology used to delineate between bodies (e.g., vagina vs. penis) and everyday ways that one acts that are culturally recognizable as gendered behavior (e.g., wearing makeup vs. not). When people have identities that deviate from societal norms (e.g., a female who has visible body hair), then others attempt to discipline them back into compliance (e.g., call her ugly). However, as many trans activists and scholars point out, many civilizations (historically and contemporarily) have more than just two gender roles, and the notion that there is an immediate correspondence between genitalia and behavior is suspect, due to the ways that people are socially, not simply biologically, conditioned to act (see Spencer & Capuzza, 2016).

The notion that people socially construct and perform their identities focuses attention on the communicative construction of identity. The belief that identity is a social, rather than simply a biological, phenomenon encourages instructors to understand and respect the students and their experiences, rituals, and habits. This ethic prompts instructors to not treat students as if the way they look immediately corresponds to their self-identification. Asking students for their preferred identity language at the beginning of the semester is one way to attend to this ethic (see Chapter 8 for activities). For example, asking students to write or talk about their preferred pronouns, such as he/she/they/ze is a great way to open conversations about gender. Furthermore, discussing the use of gendered pronouns can open fascinating conversations related to how identities are constructed through language rules. The rules provided by the Modern Language Association, for example, explicitly ban the use of "they" to refer to a singular person, despite the growing acceptance of third person pronoun use in writing to avoid sexist language. Overall, working with students to understand how identity is constituted through the dance between the cultural and individual highlights the importance of communication while prompting you to be a more sensitive instructor.

COMMITMENT 2: POWER IS FLUID AND COMPLEX

Many traditional critical theories grouped people into two camps: oppressed and privileged. Black/White, trans/cisgender, student/teacher, each of these pairs highlights the disparities between groups in terms of wealth, access, health, and other factors. Power, in this sense, is a zero-sum game—some people have it, while others do not. This view conceives of power as a material resource that can be spent to obtain goods, services, or access within society.

Although certainly such a view has the benefit of making a very pointed statement about the state of inequality between groups, it has the unfortunate tendency to simplify the complexity of injustice in ways that undermine social justice goals. For example, if a White, trans student interacts with a Black, cisgender teacher, who is the oppressed or privileged? Do we measure peoples' standing in society with an oppression calculator—plus two points for being White, but minus one for being trans? And, where are they interacting? Their identities as student/teacher are more salient in the classroom than, say, at the local gas station. These caveats, and many more, complicate the all-too-easy logic of putting people into binary pairs and invite a perspective that views power as complicated and messy.

Critical communication pedagogy draws upon the work of Black feminist scholars to recognize how power is an *intersectional* and multi-level phenomenon (Collins, 2000; Crenshaw, 1991). An intersectional understanding of power encourages instructors and students to see each other as simultaneously oppressed and privileged, due to the ways they inhabit and perform a myriad of social locations. This ethic is not to assert that people, by virtue of their dual status, are able to

> **intersectional**
> the notion that identities are not additive, but each positionality (e.g., race, gender, or sexuality) push–pull on each other to make each identity more than simply the sum of its parts.

equally exert power in every instance. Because power is also multi-level (e.g., interpersonal, institutional, and cultural), the way that people exercise power is dependent on the context in which it is negotiated. Such a view encourages you to trouble understandings of privilege and oppression by inviting a sensitive and thorough conversation about power, rather than relying on overly simplistic explanations that neglect these dynamics.

COMMITMENT 3: CULTURE IS CENTRAL, NOT ADDITIVE

We have often witnessed the unfortunate tendency of instructors to treat marginalized students as if their needs within the university are an "extra" burden. In these cases, the identity of "student" is implicitly conflated with White, middle-class, able-bodied, male students and the teaching and learning of that group is thought of as universally appropriate. Whether the instructor over-relies on lecture (which privileges a certain cognitive disposition) or physical activity (which privileges certain body types), they become frustrated when they are faced with students who cannot succeed within those narrow forms of instruction. We are often dismayed when we hear them narrate how they had to "lower their academic standards" to teach students who do not reflect the instructors' preferred method of instruction.

Critical communication pedagogy invites instructors to view teaching and learning as a cultural practice. By that we mean that your classroom instruction should not rely on a single way of teaching with concessions to so-called "alternative forms of learning" that are made grudgingly and sparingly. Rather, we believe you should strive to create a *universally designed* classroom that recognizes human variation in preferred methods of teaching and learning. For example, believing that students should verbally contribute in class or publicly disagree with an instructor demonstrates an implicit White, Western bias to classroom conduct (Hao, 2011). Rather than believing that White, Western students are "normal" and that students from Native American or East Asian cultures are "abnormal," a critical communication perspective recognizes the centrality of culture and the need to negotiate teaching and learning practices with students. Your task, as an instructor, is to recognize your own situatedness—to understand how you are the product of a particular time, history, and geography—and work to expand your instructional toolkit.

> **universally designed**
> a movement within educational studies to make curriculum, architecture, and classroom setup equally usable by all members in the classroom regardless of dis/ability. For example, providing students with text-to-speech software is a way to work toward making textbook readings universally designed.

One of the most powerful resources in the struggle to make culture central, rather than simply additive, to instruction in the classroom is your students. Students come to the classroom from a variety of different cultural locations, and with diverse cultural beliefs and opinions. If you, as an instructor, treat culture as a central concept in your own theorizing, your students are likely to take up the opportunity you are offering—making your classroom richer and more nuanced in the process.

COMMITMENT 4: CCP FOCUSES ON CONCRETE, MUNDANE COMMUNICATION PRACTICES AS CONSTITUTIVE OF LARGER STRUCTURAL SYSTEMS

How do we language others? Do we say White or Caucasian? Homosexual or Gay? Mr., Mrs., Ms., Mx.? Mainstream U.S. society, particularly political commentary, would say that these questions are simply a matter of political correctness or PC culture. In this worldview, instructors who ask for a classroom culture that is sensitive to the languaging of others are a part of the PC police. This assertion is based on the notion that language is simply a mirror for the world around us. Instructors should not sugarcoat things; they should "tell it like it is" and let PC culture be damned.

A critical communication perspective offers that the importance of communication lies in more than the immediate effect it might have in an interpersonal interaction. Rather, communication draws upon and reproduces peoples' shared understandings and builds institutional and cultural systems. For example, as we sit in meetings, talk with students, or interact with our colleagues, we often hear someone make a comment about the real world: "Students need these skills in the real world"; "In the real world, students won't get to rewrite their essays"; and "This sounds too academic. What's the payoff in the real world?" These assertions delineate between the public sector (e.g., education) and the private sector (e.g., corporations) by stating that the latter is more important or "real" than the former. Such statements, in our view, draw upon and reproduce the notion that the private sector is more important, efficient, or beneficial than public sector institutions, devaluing academic work to the role of (poor and inefficient) professional training rather than an important and unique endeavor.

While in the classroom, you will be confronted with times when you will have to identify and intervene into oppressive language practices. However, we do not think that the ethic that leads you to intervene in these situations is because an utterance "might offend someone." Such a view, in our mind, frames language use as simply an individual choice rather than a cultural practice, suggesting that it is permissible to say hateful, hurtful, or oppressive things as long as the person or group they are directed at is not present. Instead, work to recognize how your and your students' language practices can have immediate and long-term effects, and work to develop and promote a sensitive, nuanced, and evolving vocabulary about privilege and oppression—particularly as those structures manifest, and are reproduced, in our everyday communicative encounters.

COMMITMENT 5: SOCIAL, STRUCTURAL CRITIQUE CONTEXTUALIZES CONCRETE, MUNDANE COMMUNICATION PRACTICES

Closely tied to the previous commitment is the notion that instructors should be sensitive to the social and structural as a way to locate everyday language use. An excellent example of this can be found in debates about addressing *microaggressions* that occur in higher educa-tion. Mainstream media political commentary on this phenomenon derides students' stories of, or academics' research about, microaggressions. The prevailing wisdom is that students are too sensitive and that microaggres-sions are part of a culture of self-infantilization.

> **microaggressions**
> small, seemingly innocent or innocuous communicative behaviors that dominant group members direct toward marginalized group members, contributing to an ongoing culture of oppression

However, even a cursory glance at the literature about microaggressions shows that microaggressions are important to examine because they are connected to a structural system of oppression. Sue (2010) defines microaggressions as "brief, everyday exchanges that send denigrating messages to certain individuals *because of their group membership*" (p. xv, emphasis added). In other words, microaggres-sions are important because they draw upon the cultural logics that group people together and ascribe stereotypes to that identity. Pierce (1995) states that "in and of itself a microaggression may seem harmless, but the cumulative burden of a lifetime of microaggressions can theoretically contribute to diminished mortality, augmented morbidity, and flattened confidence" (p. 281). For example, although it is immediately harmful for a White speaker to ask a Latina, "Where are you from? No, really, where were you born?" because the speaker assumes she is not or cannot be U.S. American (because she is visibly darker than they are or speaks with an accent), it is the fact that she has probably encountered those questions dozens, if not hundreds of times in her life that connects it to larger systems of racism and ethnocentrism. As you facilitate class conversations, recognize that the ways your students talk in the class are more than just an expression of their individual thoughts or beliefs; instead, each utterance is made liberatory or alienating by the social systems those statements draw upon in the moment of speaking.

COMMITMENT 6: LANGUAGE (AND ANALYSIS OF LANGUAGE) IS CENTRAL TO CCP

Although it might seem to be self-evident that communication scholars should research and teach about language, the sad fact is that much of our disciplinary history is characterized by theories, frameworks, and concepts from psychology, sociology, and business administration (Craig, 1998). Certainly, there is something to be learned from an *interdisciplinary* perspective, and incorporating the findings of other disciplines can help push new ideas within the field. However, we strongly

> **interdisciplinary**
> relating to more than one discipline

believe that communication scholars have something unique to offer about discussions about language and that it is our disciplinary responsibility to advance knowledge within that framework.

As you teach your communication courses, we ask you to think about how you talk to students about the importance of communication in their lives. Is it simply a way to express one's thoughts? An instrument used to persuade others? Or, maybe a skill that can be practiced, mastered, and "sold" to the highest bidder? We argue that language is central to the human condition, that beyond our opposable thumbs and bipedal legs, it is our ability to be symbol-manipulating creatures that makes us distinct from (although not more important than) other species. As communication scholars, we encourage you to discuss with students the need for studying communication beyond its immediate worth as a tool to accrue more wealth or access. Rather, how can our study of language help people articulate the value of community, forgiveness, humility, and justice in an age of gross inequality and alienation?

COMMITMENT 7: REFLEXIVITY IS AN ESSENTIAL CONDITION FOR CCP

Reflexivity, according to Freire (2000), is an ethical commitment to critically reflect on one's positionality and be accountable to those people who instructors purport to serve. The term encourages instructors to go beyond mere reflection and only thinking about one's own actions, and instead to think about one's thinking, to recognize the limits of one's imagination. For example, a reflective teacher may ask, "Did I engage in effective instruction to students?" However, a reflexive teacher may ask, "Did the content students learned today reflect my biases or the biases of dominant interests?" In the latter question, the question of effective instruction is encompassed within a much more pressing question: Whose knowledge counts as "real" or "true" knowledge? Being a reflexive instructor means that you work to recognize, in relation to students, the ways that dominant knowledges influence your teaching—your methods of instruction, ways of giving feedback, or thinking when choosing course texts. As a critical endeavor, it demands that you go beyond merely recognizing your situatedness to actively and intentionally work to decenter dominant ways of being or knowing in the world.

The concept of reflexivity is closely tied to the concept of *voice* or the ability of people, as individuals or as groups, to speak about, and in the language of, their cultural or experiential knowledge. When people are not reflexive, they may believe that everyone's voice competes in the marketplace of ideas—a neutral territory where the best idea always wins. However, we assert that ideas win (or become or stay dominant) based mainly on how they appeal to the interests of dominant groups. For example, the reason that substantial conversations about race, class, sexuality, and gender are rare in higher education is because dominant groups do not want, know how, and/or care to have those conversations take place.

voice
the ability of people, as individuals or as groups, to speak about, and in the language of, their cultural or experiential knowledge

Although some people may argue that a social justice education is supposed to "give voice to the voiceless," we push back against this understanding. Every group, no matter how marginalized, has a voice to speak about their experiences. However, dominant groups often do not listen when marginalized people speak. Saying that marginalized people are "voiceless" confuses this relationship and makes it appear as if the problem lies with oppressed groups who need privileged groups' help or charity. A reflexive instructor recognizes the need to listen to others and, concomitantly, the need to create or give up a space for marginalized voices to be heard and taken seriously. For example, in a public speaking class you are likely to show example speeches from a variety of sources. Incorporating texts from outside of the dominant terrain of public political speeches can open additional space for your class to reflect on the variety of ways that public speaking manifests and helps shape public discussions.

COMMITMENT 8: CCP EDUCATORS EMBRACE PEDAGOGY AND RESEARCH AS PRAXIS

Teaching and research can often feel like solitary endeavors. Instructors spend hours reading texts, searching for relevant examples, and crafting lesson outlines to create compelling classroom environments. Similarly, researchers spend hours in coffee shops, libraries, and home offices writing, editing, and reading. Sometimes it is hard to see either form of work as a space for collaboration. Many people think that being asked to change their methods of instruction or to revise a paper is a personal attack or an indication that they are doing something wrong, bad, or stupid. Such thinking makes it difficult to talk about how to improve ourselves and the world around us because we privilege our bruised egos over doing the hard and heart work of changing.

A CCP perspective asserts that teaching and research are mutually informing, encompassing what Freire (2000) calls praxis. As hooks (1994) stated, "I came to theory because I was hurting" (p. 59). In other words, there is value in finding knowledge and a community that address the issues we all face as social justice educators and activists. Teachers must be grounded in more than their subjective preferences for instruction; rather, they should continuously strive to improve their craft. Developing, not just reading, others' research puts your ideas into conversation with other members of field, ensuring that your methods, vocabularies, and content reflect the best advances of the discipline. At the same time, your teaching should inform your research. The difficulties, triumphs, and conundrums you encounter as a teacher are the things you can theorize about through your research (an ethic we try to live out in the writing of this book!). Both research and teaching, within this framework, are constantly improved through the process of engaging in conversations with others in your scholarly community.

COMMITMENT 9: CCP EDUCATORS EMBRACE A NUANCED UNDERSTANDING OF SUBJECTIVITY AND AGENCY

Can individuals actually challenge and change inequality? This is perhaps one of the most vexing conundrums for social justice scholars. Some scholars argue that overcoming oppressive systems is simply an illusion and that capitalism, racism, genderism (or other oppressive social systems) are unchanged by individuals' actions. Others scholars assert that resistance can be found in the most mundane of social practices and valorize those moments beyond their social significance. In both instances, scholars' conversations revolve around issues of *subjectivity* (i.e., performing one's self) and *agency* (i.e., the ability to change social circumstances).

subjectivity

the ability of people, as individuals or as groups, to perform their identity

agency

the ability of people, as individuals or as groups, to change their circumstances

Critical commination pedagogy tries to navigate between the "rock and a hard place" of these two ways of thinking about social relationships. Individual identities are the result, in part, of cultural systems that people are born into and have little influence over in a systemic sense. Race, gender, dis/ability, and other identity markers were around long before we were born and will persist long after we are gone. However, due to the conflicting and complementary ways that cultural systems interact, individuals have the creative capacity to change their own and society's social circumstances. For example, what it means to be female in the United States has changed dramatically over the past 200 years due to the ways that feminists have called into question patriarchal norms by appealing to other systems, such as democracy, individualism, and equality. How people perform their femaleness, and the changes they enact around them, are shaped and constrained by the time and place they are in, but they are not determined or mandated by those circumstances.

As a social justice instructor, embracing this ethic will help you talk about privilege and oppression in ways that go beyond mere charity. We remember, and wince, when we first became interested in social justice and thought that our mission was to help those in need. As we continue to strive and improve our activism, we recognize that such an ethic denies peoples' subjectivity and bars their agency. Although certainly there are times when others need help, you shouldn't treat students, or teach students to view others, as if they are deficit to your understanding of the world or in need of your help. Rather, you should try to engender a collaborative ethic—one where you and students engage in the activity of joint discovery of the ways to understand, confront, and change oppressive social constraints.

COMMITMENT 10: DIALOGUE IS METAPHOR AND METHOD FOR OUR RELATIONSHIPS WITH OTHERS

CCP exhorts instructors and students to engage in dialogue as way to challenge taken-for-granted assumptions and act to change them (Freire, 2000; Kahl, 2013). Fassett and Warren (2007) define dialogue as "a process of sensitive and thorough inquiry, inquiry we undertake together to (de)construct ideologies, identities, and cultures" (p. 55). Dialogue, in this sense, is an intentional communicative practice that is realized when two or more individuals strive to name, challenge, and transform oppressive systems. Dialogue is not just a "good conversation" and it is definitely not the uncritical acceptance of other's ideas—it can and most likely will be a messy, emotional, and painful process of discovery for all involved.

As you strive to practice a social justice ethic within the classroom, one of the challenges is how to engage in dialogue with students about privilege and oppression. Although we talk about the pitfalls of dialogue in Chapter 6, we want to address this concern here as well. There will be times when students say and do things in the classroom that will break your heart, make you scratch your head, or wonder if your class has any value at all. There will also be times when talk about issues such as race, class, or gender will make students feel threatened and defensive about the ways they normally interact with others. Your task as an instructor is to attempt to create the conditions for students to substantially engage with issues of privilege and oppression. However, you cannot force them to adopt your beliefs, as such an ethic is a form of violence. As Freire (2000) asserts, violence cannot be used to overcome oppression; rather, creating communities of love and hope offers the opportunity for substantial, ongoing, and positive change in society through the power of sustained, thoughtful, and reflexive dialogue.

CONCLUSION

Critical communication pedagogy provides a framework from which teachers and researchers can articulate a vision for the classroom and society that is radically hopeful. We believe students and teachers can learn ways of being in the world that go beyond simply learning the best way to give a speech or effective ways of interacting interpersonally to encompass questions about power, identity, context, and inequality. We also assert that our teaching and scholarship should be dedicated to the goal of realizing ways to create communities that (in both process and product) affirm peoples' worth and allow "all humans to live in societies [that] provide the conditions necessary to allow people 'to do' and 'to be'" (Pyles, 2014, p. 6). In other words, to create a (global) society where people are free to live to the full extent of their capabilities without the intrusion of oppressive social or material structures.

As you work to adopt a social justice perspective on teaching, we hope that the 10 commitments can help you develop a sensitive, nuanced, and hopeful approach to classroom instruction. You have an incredible amount of responsibility: classroom management, grading, taking attendance, creating a syllabus, facilitating discussion, and much, much more. It may feel like social justice is just another duty, another box that needs to be ticked off in your quest to cover ground in your class. However, we believe social justice, as practiced through CCP, is central rather than additive to classroom pedagogy. And, in the following chapters, we outline the issues that faced and continue to challenge us as instructors, in the hope that you can learn from our stories and push for a socially just world.

Journal/Discussion Questions

1. What are ways that you can make critical communication pedagogy central to teaching communication (i.e., communication education) or teaching in general (i.e., instructional communication)?
2. What constitutes the study of "communication" in educational spaces?
3. Do you agree with each of the 10 commitments? Why or why not?
4. Would you add any commitments to critical communication pedagogy? Explain.
5. How do you see the 10 commitments changing your classroom practice, syllabus construction, or course material choices?

3

POSITIONING/ORIENTING TOWARD THE COMMUNICATION CLASSROOM

THE CLASSROOMS IN OUR LIVES ARE NOT PLAY—TEACHERS AND STUDENTS LEAVE FINGERPRINTS ON THE LIVES THEY TOUCH IN PEDAGOGICAL SETTINGS, PERCEPTIBLE IMPRESSIONS THAT WILL HAVE LASTING EFFECTS ON US. WE ARE FOOLING OURSELVES TO IMAGINE THEM HAPPENING IN ANY OTHER WAY.

FASSETT AND WARREN (2007, PP. 70–71)

IT IS TWO MONTHS BEFORE I START MY DOCTORAL PROGRAM. I am still finishing up my thesis as I get ready to make the move to Southern Illinois University in Carbondale. I am excited and nervous, but, most of all, I am exhausted. Wrapping up course work, writing chapters, and presenting papers at the Central States Communication Association conference have taken their toll.

I look around my tiny apartment. Soon, I'll be saying goodbye to the little two-bedroom that has been my home for two years now. The brown carpet is old and stained, but feels fluffy and warm under my bare feet. I walk out of my apartment and downstairs to get my mail. As I flip through the credit card offers and flyers, I find a large manila envelope with SIU's return address on it. A bolt of fear shoots through me. "What if they say they made a mistake and that I'm not really accepted?" I think to myself. I walk back upstairs to my apartment so I can open it without anyone else watching me.

I put the envelope on the coffee table in the living room and try to forget about it. I decide that I'll clean my apartment first, and then I'll read the message. All day as I clean I can see the envelope sitting on the coffee table, watching, waiting, like a snake. Finally, I can't take it anymore and I rush over to the envelope and rip it open. I scan the first page of a thick bunch of documents and read the top of the first page: "Congratulations on your acceptance! We hope your summer is going well. Enclosed are materials that you should read before GTA Orientation. Remember, orientation is the week prior to the beginning of the semester. Attendance is mandatory."

*****

What kind of preparation did you receive before teaching your first class? Did your department give you a packet of readings and a week-long training seminar? Or, did they hand you a book and tell you to "sink or swim"? Regardless of your department's approach to teaching you how to be an instructor, we believe that training gives insights into the kind of culture that you are going to be a part of for the next few years of your life. Rather than viewing the documents, seminars, and training sessions as a burden on your time and attention, we argue that these practices provide important insights into how your department values you and your pedagogy.

One way that we can understand the amalgamation of rules and rituals in your department is to think of them as a culture of power (Delpit, 1988). Delpit articulates five tenets in her explanation of the culture of power:

1. Issues of power are enacted in classrooms.
2. There are codes or rules for participating in power; that is, there is a "culture of power."
3. The rules of the culture of power are a reflection of the rules of the culture of those who have power.
4. If you are not already a participant in the culture of power, being told explicitly the rules of that culture makes acquiring power easier.
5. Those with power are frequently least aware of—or least willing to acknowledge—its existence. Those with less power are often most aware of its existence. (p. 282)

The ways that your department treats you and your pedagogical choices is not happenstance. Rituals, such as sending a packet of reading materials, are practices that were most likely enacted for many years before you enrolled and will continue after you have gone. In other words, they constitute a constellation of meanings that help you know what is (un)important about your teaching: multiple choice tests versus essays, lecture versus activity-based instruction, or an individualized versus collaborative climate. As Kathryn found out after reading the materials, knowing your departmental culture can provide you with insights into how you are expected to conduct yourself as a teaching professional and, just as important, where you can take up, resist, defer, or subvert those expectations. We know that departmental culture can vary greatly from institution to institution, so utilize the advice we offer in conjunction with rules and norms of the place you work within.

For us, this different cultural orientation towards teaching was obvious in the different ways that we learned how to be teachers between our master's and PhD programs. As MA students, we received as little as a three-day crash course in teaching at our various institutions. Our training primarily covered questions of how to maintain our authority in the classroom, and how to deal with problem students. Leaving that training, we knew that our departments were concerned with making sure that material was covered in a satisfactory way, and that classroom management was the primary evidence of "good teaching." When we entered our PhD program, we experienced a week-long orientation, and a mandatory class about teaching. From this perspective, our duties as a teacher were important to our development as academics. We were expected to be thoughtful and reflective about our instruction and to engage in collaboration and dialogue rather than direct instruction. Although we deeply appreciated both approaches, and the fact that we received formal education in our teaching strategies at both institutions, the culture of power that developed was profoundly different in each location. The expectations of what made a "successful semester" were highly dependent on the culture developed in each department.

As you think about what kind of department you are in and (just as important) what kind of teacher you want to be, we encourage you to flip this lens onto your teaching practices. How do your expectations about instruction reflect your own biases? And, most importantly, how do your biases serve to create a culture of power in the classroom? We believe that because many instructors have been successful students, it is sometimes difficult for them to recognize the way their biases (re)produce the culture of power in the classroom. Instead of finding various ways of teaching, many instructors simply rely on the way that they prefer to learn, without recognizing that there is no one-size-fits-all to instruction. Furthermore, some (un)intentionally overvalue the knowledges of dominant people, *alienating* students from their ability to be transformative change agents. These concerns are particularly salient when an instructor identifies with dominant cultural positions (e.g., White, heterosexual, and/or male). In this chapter, we encourage instructors to become intentional in their efforts to demystify the culture of power and their culpability in its maintenance. We use this framework to talk about issues that arise in the first few weeks of the semester (or even before it begins!), such as syllabus construction, course materials, and dress codes.

> **alienate**
> to make a person feel isolated, disconnected, or estranged from their own sense of self and/or others

SYLLABUS CONSTRUCTION

Whether your syllabus is self or departmentally generated, we believe that syllabus construction and presentation is an important classroom ritual. Thompson (2007) offers that the syllabus introduces three important challenges to instructors: 1) balancing the tension between being viewed as caring and yet rigorous; 2) negotiating how much personal (i.e., teaching philosophy) and rules-oriented (e.g., attendance policy) information to include; and 3) finding ways to encourage students to read, retain, and revisit the information in the syllabus. We frame these concerns within our concept of the culture of power; that is, we argue that the syllabus should be viewed as an opportunity to make explicit and intentional choices about the classroom culture. Thus, the syllabus can be an opportunity to co-construct a classroom atmosphere that affirms the lived experiences of students.

We believe the syllabus can be a conversation starter about the culture of power. The syllabus can provide a space for you to articulate and negotiate your expectations for class behavior. For example, many instructors have policies regarding turning in late work. Some instructors take a number of points off for each day an assignment is late (e.g., deducting 10 points per day), while others simply do not accept late work. But, a correct answer is correct on Tuesday and Friday, so why do we differentiate based on the day that the answer is turned in to us? Many instructors may respond that students need to learn how to work in the "real world." They appeal to the experiences of those in the private sector to defend their choice as practical and pragmatic.

We take issue with this kind of response for two reasons. First, although we certainly want students to be able to succeed within and beyond college, and recognize that time management is a component of that success, to act as if everyone should operate within this mentality privileges corporate culture. In other words, it *normalizes* corporate culture by acting as if corporate time is the most logical or common-sense approach to viewing time management. Second, it elides instructors' responsibility to be explicit and intentional about the culture of power. Instructors have the ability to negotiate whatever time management system they want with students within the classroom. To act as if time management rules are beyond their power to change by appealing to the real world obfuscates how much power they have in the class.

> **normalize**
> to make a culturally arbitrary value (e.g., liking chocolate ice cream) seem normal, thus marginalizing other values (e.g., liking vanilla ice cream) so they seem silly, foolish, or dangerous

We offer that the primary reason instructors have due dates for assignments is because it makes grading more efficient and thus easier for the teacher. From this insight we can conclude that instructors should not view due dates as inherently good or necessary, but a site of negotiation and collaboration. Perhaps you create a student contract where students decide what assignments they want and when to turn them in, or maybe you provide those rules to students with a little chance for student input. Although we hope that you use the syllabus as a place to share power with students, we believe that (at minimum) you should be open and honest with students about your expectations and own up to the fact that they are *your* expectations.

Rather than viewing the syllabus as an immutable contract, we argue that it should be a way to start conversations by making parts or all of it open for student-led change. This approach to syllabus construction can be messy and threatening for even the most seasoned teacher. Many instructors believe that letting students create their own due dates, assign points to tests or quizzes, or set up class decorum rules is akin to letting the fox guard the henhouse. However, we argue that if instructors want students to cultivate a democratic, collaborative, and empowered identity, then they must model those principles in their classroom teaching.

We do not mean to imply that every part of the syllabus must be up for negotiation. As Freire (1994) cautions, instructors should not act as if simply ceding all power in the classroom is inherently liberatory. To force students to make all of the decisions about the class is an abdication of your responsibility as an educator and a mystification of the culture of power. However, we argue that the syllabus should be viewed as a living document that can be nurtured and sustained through student and instructor input. For example, you may ask students to develop a list of classroom rules for interaction to ensure that students respect each other's contributions during discussion. This type of activity encourages students to interact with one another, deliberate about the types of rules they want, and negotiate their personal desires with those of the group. By encouraging students to take control of their learning, you create the conditions for students to realize their capacity as creative, empowered agents in the class.

We have offered in this section that the syllabus should be viewed as a conversation starter rather than a closer. To aid you, we have provided a sample syllabus (see Appendix A) for an Introduction to Communication Studies Course. We also encourage you, if you or someone you know are a member of the National Communication Association, to visit the association's syllabus repository (http://natcom.org/Tertiary.aspx?id=180). This resource has multiple syllabi for dozens of different communication courses. Whether you adapt a syllabus from us, the NCA website, somewhere else, or create your own, you should never feel that a syllabus is written in stone. Although certainly changing the syllabus every week may be disorienting to students (how can you make the culture of power explicit when you always change it?), slavishly adhering to the syllabus is often a recipe for disaster. Listen to your students. If they seem to be struggling to keep up with the readings or assignments, then perhaps you have misjudged your audience. Asking students for their feedback and input on the syllabus throughout the semester is an excellent way to make sure that you are in tune with the needs of your students. Furthermore, it encourages students to revisit the syllabus and remember important dates and assignments because you are continually submitting syllabus material for revision.

heterosexism

beliefs, norms, and attitudes, operating at all levels of society and with(out) conscious intent, that normalize opposite-sex desire, affect, and relationships and reinforce the subjugation of non-opposite sex desire, affect, and relationships (e.g., pansexual, same-sex, and asexual)

ethnocentrism

the belief that one's culture is superior to others' culture

COURSE MATERIALS

Perhaps the most common type of course material in higher education is the textbook. Research concerning textbooks reveals two important insights. First, students often believe that textbooks are credible sources of unbiased information (McGarrity, 2010; Robson, 2001). Second, past studies examining textbooks have shown they often function to promote *heterosexism* (Myerson, Crawley, Anstey, Kessler, & Okopny, 2007), *ethnocentrism* (Matveeva, 2007), and dis/ableism (Johnson & Nieto, 2007). These two insights should encourage you to identify and challenge the ways that your course texts may teach students oppressive "educational ideals" (Gullicks, Pearson, Child, & Schwab, 2005, p. 249). As we become more firmly entrenched in the media age, we want to remind you that materials do not have to be just textbooks; rather, they can include video clips, newspaper articles, journal articles, poems, or songs. Considering how instructors select and use course materials, as well as what type of material you choose to include as a course text, is an important way to identify and challenge the culture of power in the classroom.

One way that teachers can work to dismantle the culture of power is to provide alternatives to its assumed normalcy. Whether the textbook you utilize focuses on social justice issues or not, we believe you should include additional texts to expand the types of knowledge that students have access to in the class. No singular text (no matter how engaging) can possibly encapsulate all of the *cultures* that reflect our society. For example, one text may focus on race, another on gender, and a third might use an intersectional focus to talk about gendered racism. However, you should strive to talk about all forms of oppression, including ageism, classism, dis/ableism, genderism, racism, and sexism (to name a few).

> **culture**
> a system of beliefs, attitudes, and behaviors that are communicatively enacted, taken up, resisted, deferred, and subverted within a particular time and place

> **queer**
> a word traditionally used to shame or attack non-heterosexual desire (e.g., pansexual, same-sex, or bisexual); many (although not all) LGBTQ people have sought to reclaim the word as a political act

One insidious way that instructors unwittingly perpetuate the culture of power is by talking about privilege and oppression, but only using course texts from traditionally privileged perspectives. You should strive to talk about oppressive systems from the viewpoints of traditionally marginalized groups. Is it important that White men talk about gendered racism? Yes! But, if they are the only ones that are listened to then it continues the marginalization of voices of oppressed people, such as *queer* women of color. One strategy is to find texts that fall outside of pre-conceived notions of texts; for example, assigning students to listen to and consider a hip hop CD, or using an afrofuturist science fiction author like Octavia Butler to discuss communication constructs. By intentionally and explicitly including the voices of marginalized people within your course, you decenter yourself as the sole authority and provide alternatives to the normalcy of dominant perspectives on history and communication.

When you provide a range of course texts, you should be prepared for some students to have difficulty appreciating texts that are outside of their comfort zone. Many students may not have experience reading languages, dialects, or organizational patterns that do not adhere to the strictures of White, middle-class, and linear representations. You will need to develop the ability distinguish between students' unwillingness to read and their struggle with course texts. Some students may not have the *cultural capital* to appreciate some formats fully, but excel in others (Yosso, 2005). At the same time, other students may resist having to engage with texts because they do not want to give up the privilege of having every text given to them in their preferred style of representation. Overall, it is important that texts that you choose do not simply fill a quota system of marginalized voices (i.e., tokenism), but encourage students to explore their identity and create meaningful discussions about privilege and oppression.

> **cultural capital**
> the implicit mental frameworks that people utilize to navigate institutions; in the United States, the more cultural capital one has, the more they are able to perform in ways that correspond to middle/upper class White culture

Another way to displace the culture of power is to solicit student input on the course text selections. Although you most likely will not be able to select a different textbook mid-semester, there are ways to ensure that students have an active role in creating the direction and tone of the course. For example, you can ask students to bring in music videos, YouTube clips, or newspaper articles that connect to the class reading for the day. Although this task seems simplistic on the surface, when the topics of class revolve around privilege and oppression the effects can be inspiring. Student in our classes often bring in texts such as video clips that show protests against anti-Black violence on college campuses, slam poetry that critiques sexism, and newspaper articles that highlight damaging tropes about trans folk. Students have a wealth of knowledge at their disposal, and their knowledge is often more up to date with current cultural trends and pop culture than your own. As an instructor, it is your job to help them make sense of their knowledge within a social justice framework. By utilizing their contributions, you can affirm their interests, which helps make the course more relevant to their lived experiences.

The approach to course materials in a class can have a great deal of influence on how you identify and challenge the culture of power. As with anything else in the classroom, make sure to talk with students about the choices regarding the selection and incorporation of course texts, and be open to student feedback. Additionally, be aware of how textbook costs may prevent or restrict student access. Encouraging reading and discussion groups, putting textbooks on course reserve at your library, and allowing students to use your textbook are all ways to ensure that students have access to the materials used in class. Finally, we believe that making the culture of power a topic of conversation in the classroom can encourage students to engage in course texts. Many of our colleagues lament that their students do not read class materials. Although there is certainly no magic bullet that will ensure complete reading participation, our experiences lead us to believe that curriculum is too often removed from their lived experiences. Students who help create the classroom culture through course texts have a greater investment in the course curriculum and therefore often exhibit a greater likelihood to engage in course content.

DRESS CODES

The way instructors dress is a matter of personal preference, functionality, and (dis)conformity to institutional rules. Oftentimes, instructors utilize dress as a way to manage student impressions about their personality (see Goffman, 1959). Although some might find the topic of attire to be pedantic, we offer that attire in the classroom can be an important yet overlooked element that can perpetuate a culture of power. In this section, we first review literature concerning instructor attire in order to offer some advice. We then interrogate how research has given a prescriptive view of attire that does not adequately attend to class, gender, race, and sexuality, in order to explode the seemingly common-sense advice concerning instructor attire.

Researchers within and beyond the communication discipline have paid a great deal of time examining how students' perceptions of instructors change due to attire (e.g., Carr, Davies, & Lavin, 2010; Gorham, Cohen, & Morris, 1999; Roach, 1997). After reviewing the literature in this area, we believe that your attire should reflect the type of persona that you wish to cultivate or the type of credibility that you wish to enhance. For example, Morris, Gorham, Cohen, and Huffman (1996) found that students rated instructors higher on reports of competence when they dressed in traditional attire (e.g., dark business suit for men, dark skirted business suit for women). However, students thought the instructors were more extroverted, sociable, and interesting when dressed in casual attire (e.g., faded blue jeans and T-shirt for men and women). In other words, if you feel that students may question your competence, then dressing in professional attire may mitigate their biases. On the other hand, if you feel that you may have trouble connecting with your students on a relational level, perhaps dressing in a casual fashion may help. Making sure that your attire presents the type of persona that you wish to cultivate is an important step in being an authentic and honest instructor.

Although there is certainly advice to be given about clothing, we also wish to interrogate this seemingly mundane practice in order to highlight the culture of power. Your attire is a cultural practice that draws upon and *reifies* societal norms and rules. Although some teachers, and students, may argue that all instructors should dress casually in order to mitigate the balance of power between students and instructors, this type of assertion treats all instructors as if they share the same level of power and respect. For example, female scholars of color argue that their credibility in the classroom is often questioned, and that they often dress in professional attire as a way to combat negative cultural stereotypes (Sulé, 2010). Their critique shows that simply trading one culture of power (e.g., everyone should wear traditional clothing) for another (e.g., everyone should wear casual clothing) is not a solution rooted in *praxis*, but is a prescription that often caters to people from dominant positions in society.

> **reify**
> to act as if something is concrete or real when it is a social construction

One way that one can see how attire is a powerful yet mundane part of identity performance is to understand the role of attire when instructors identify as *genderqueer*. As an observant reader may have noticed from the research we related above, studies often treat males and females as a discrete binary. However, gendered experiences are not so neatly encapsulated in a male/female dichotomy. Many genderqueer folk may or may not try to dress in ways to pass—that is, in ways that match dominant cultural codes about their perceived gender—while others may find passing a heterosexist, cisgendered

> **genderqueer**
> a person who does not subscribe to typical male/female or masculine/feminine gender scripts; a person can adopt both, a combination, or none of these positions

burden. These decisions are loaded, and instructors should carefully consider how their choices will affect them in the classroom. For example, Kyle C. has been told in previous institutions to avoid coming out as gay, or genderqueer, in the classroom because that revelation could negatively affect his teaching evaluations. Although he chooses to regularly disclose his identities in the classroom, he does not feel comfortable dressing in ways that affirm his identity in the classroom.

Recognizing the messiness of dress can be an important starting point for conversations about privilege and oppression. For example, Kyle Rudick enjoys interacting with students, and wears blue jeans and an untucked button-up almost every day in order to lessen the power distance between him and his students. However, the fact that he can choose to wear professional or casual clothing derives from his privilege as a White, cisgender, male instructor. His authority is very seldom openly challenged in class because he embodies many of the cultural norms of authority. Kyle R. often uses his body and clothing as an opening for conversation about privilege and oppression in class, asking students to think about how his use of clothing reflects and reproduces societal norms about what a "professor" should look like in the classroom. Encouraging students to focus on the everyday, mundane ways that people perform gender, race, and class can help instructors guide students toward unpacking assumptions about how bodies should or should not present in order to be viewed as "normal."

Although we have had success opening up these conversations, we cannot in good consciousness exhort you to always strive for the same level of openness in this matter. For many instructors from marginalized positions, the very act of bringing up their identity may invite student resistance or even violence. One way that you might talk about attire is to bring up the topic in the abstract or with visual aids based on popular culture before inviting students into a conversation about the instructor's choice of clothing. Overall, the ordinariness of clothing makes it an important area to talk about in order to interrogate the seemingly commonsensical practices of the culture of power.

CONCLUSION

In this chapter, we have utilized Delpit's (1988) notion of the culture of power to highlight how privilege and oppression can be identified and challenged in the classroom. Specifically, we offer that seemingly mundane practices such as syllabus construction, course texts, and attire can be important sites for investigation and conversation. As you begin to create or edit your course materials, we hope that you will find ways to open conversations with your students in order to demystify the seeming normalcy of classroom culture.

As you move forward with your teaching, remember that you will be spending many weeks or months with the students in your classes. Every interaction that you have with them, no matter how seemingly trivial, has the potential to create and sustain a culture of power in the classroom. It is your job to use the classroom as a laboratory of sorts; that is, by working with students to help them develop their critical capacity to interrogate classroom practices, you help them hone those skills for other areas of criticism in their lives. For example, discussing the politics of attire in the classroom can be an excellent way to introduce topics of sexism or racism in advertising or movies. Your responsibility to your students is to model the kind of conversation you wish people in society were having about privilege and oppression.

Journal/Discussion Questions

1. As a student, in what ways did syllabi help or restrict your ability to be successful in your past college courses?
2. As an instructor, how would you create syllabi documents that are the most helpful to your younger student self?
3. How will you ensure that the texts and materials you use in class will be inclusive for non-dominant group members?
4. How will you make decisions with your students about the course material and texts?
5. How do you understand performing your teacher identity through attire?
   a. What would you never choose to wear as a social justice teacher? Why?
   b. What attire would make you more inviting to your students? Why?

ASSESSMENT AND POWER IN THE COMMUNICATION CLASSROOM

WE WILL SEE EXPLORATIONS OF ASSESSMENT, OF HOW WE CAN KNOW EFFORTS TOWARD CRITICAL COMMUNICATION PEDAGOGY ARE, INDEED, SUCCESSFUL IN, FOR EXAMPLE, CULTIVATING REFLEXIVITY; CRITICAL COMMUNICATION EDUCATORS ARE ALSO LIKELY TO EXAMINE AND ASK INCLUSIVE QUESTIONS REGARDING THE NATURE AND POLITICS OF UNDEREXPLORED APPROACHES TO ASSESSMENT.

FASSETT AND WARREN (2007, P. 289)

TODAY IS THE FIRST DAY THAT I GET TO TEACH A COLLEGE CLASS. As I walk toward the classroom, I realize that I forgot the copies of the course syllabus, so I run back to my office. The combination of an 8:00 a.m. class time and my lack of sleep due to nerves has stripped what little organizational powers I have. I pick up copies off my desk and head back down to the classroom, walking a little faster this time. I don't want to be late and give the students a bad first impression.

"Hello everyone!" I say as I enter the classroom, a big smile on my face. I get a few half-hearted greetings in return. Many of the students are still wearing pajama pants, hats, and other attire that shows they came to class almost immediately after waking up that morning. "Tough crowd," I think. I continue, out loud, "We're going to go over the course syllabus and then do an icebreaker activity to get to know each other a bit better," as I hand out copies of the syllabus. I try to keep my voice cheerful and ask questions as I walk around the room. After a few minutes some of the students start to reciprocate and I can tell the whole class is a little more enthusiastic than when I first entered the room.

I begin the class by pointing out parts of the syllabus that are open for negotiation and change. I explain that some parts of the class, such as the textbook we will use, are beyond my control, but that I would like their input on class rules and assignment scheduling. I break students into small groups to discuss the syllabus and that's when I realize I have to use the restroom. Bad. I look up at the clock and (to my horror) I realize that only 15 minutes have passed. There's still almost an hour of class left.

I try to do things to distract myself. I walk around. Still have to go. I talk to students in their groups. Not better. I try to reread the syllabus. Nope. I sit down. Definitely worse. As I shift my weight from side to side like a 4-year-old who has to "go potty," a student raises his hand. "Yeah, Walter. What's up?" I pant, perspiration beading on my face.

He looks at me with an embarrassed smile, "Can I use the restroom, please?"

****

The hidden curriculum (Giroux & Penna, 1983) refers to the values and norms that are transferred through their perceived normalcy. Every semester, we have students in class ask us to use the restroom. Why? The most likely explanation is that (from kindergarten to college) they have been taught that the teacher is in control of the classroom and therefore students' bodies. Students learn math, science, and language, but (above all) they learn to rely upon and acquiesce to the instructor (Gatto, 2006). As Kyle R.'s narrative illustrates, even when students become teachers, they often continue to follow the hidden curriculum. We become so wrapped up in acting like an authority in the classroom that we forget that teachers are humans with human needs, affects, and desires. Such a view shows that the hidden curriculum does more than simply teach students how to behave in the classroom; it creates an expectation for what is normal or appropriate behavior that endures beyond the context where it was learned.

Of course, the hidden curriculum is far more encompassing than just restroom time. Each and every one of the daily rituals that constitute the practice of education serves to draw upon and reproduce the hidden curriculum: turn taking, raising hands for permission to speak, seat arrangement, and the choice of class texts are just some examples of the ways that values and norms are implicitly taught within institutions of higher education. Importantly, the hidden curriculum is not only a matter of teachers enforcing their will upon students. Instructors are also socialized into valuing certain behaviors or norms over others through day-to-day interactions in the classroom. It is important that you cultivate an ethic of reflection in order to avoid the risk of (un)intentionally passing oppressive hidden lessons on to students.

The concept of the hidden curriculum is useful when examining the role of *assessment* in education. Rather than believing that grading, tests, and essays are natural or obligatory practices within higher education, we believe that viewing assessment as a part of the hidden curriculum challenges us to imagine possibilities for its transformation. Although certainly some critical scholars believe that all assessment is oppressive and should be dismantled (e.g., Barros, 2011), we are persuaded by Kahl's (2013) challenge to undo restrictive ways of thinking about the relationship between assessment and critical teaching by articulating transformative practices at their intersection. As Knight (2011) articulates,

> One of my greatest fears as an educator has been that if we don't develop our own measures for ensuring that what we do works and why, then surely someone else will do it for us—and most likely someone without our expertise. (p. 246)

Indeed, it is exactly because assessment is viewed as natural, and the exercise of power through grading is so normal, that social justice–minded educators should develop critically informed and culturally sensitive forms of assessment. Important to this process is the demand that critical assignments and assessment must unmask the hidden curriculum (both within and outside of the classroom) as their process and product. As process, course assignments should be explicit and open to negotiation (see Chapter 3). As product, the result of engaging in critical coursework should be a critical awareness of how privilege and oppression become normalized through our everyday interactions. In this chapter, we reimagine public speeches, essays, and portfolios as three types of assessment can become sites of negotiation and collaboration. Our advice is rooted in our experiences teaching at universities with class caps of 30 or

assessment
the act of ascertaining whether a stated objective was met through instruction

less students. As such, if you work at a university with a large lecture format, you may need to adapt our advice to be manageable to your time and energy.[1]

PUBLIC SPEECHES

The teaching of public speaking is arguably one of the most important missions of our discipline. In fact, public speaking pedagogy was one of the main reasons that the first speech teachers broke away from the English discipline in order to form what is now known as communication studies (Gehrke & Keith, 2015). Verderber (1991) offers that introductory courses that focus on teaching public speaking skills should teach students how to

> learn to select topics, write speech goals, analyze audiences and occasions, discover and create supporting material, state and organize main points, create introductions and conclusions, and develop a personal, effective speaking style that includes effective use of language and delivery. (p. 4)

Implicit in his list of objectives is a notion that public speaking is a tool, one that is neither inherently good nor bad, but that is either effective or ineffective. We believe that such a view of public speaking constitutes a type of hidden curriculum; that is, it implicitly foregrounds skills over ethics. We do not view public speaking as a neutral "skill" that can be used for either positive or negative ends, but one that should be taught with a social justice ethic at its core. Although we certainly agree that learning what constitutes (in)effectual public speaking is important, we argue that public speaking is made meaningful when students and instructors understand its potential for social justice advocacy. In this section, we offer some ways that instructors and students can explore public speaking as a way to challenge and change privilege and oppression.

---

1   We chose these types of assignments because they are culturally recognizable and institutionally sanctioned forms of assessment that are open to renegotiation and change. We believe that traditional forms of assessment (e.g., multiple choice tests) have very limited potential to foster thoughtful or meaningful engagement with topics concerning privilege and oppression.

One of the most important components of teaching public speaking as an act of social justice advocacy is encouraging students to address topics that deal with privilege and oppression. Teaching students the mechanics of public speaking can be accomplished by giving them topics that are artificial or banal. However, if you believe that public speaking should be taught in ways that help students cultivate an ethic of responsibility to improve the communities they are a part of, then you must connect their public speaking to the cultural systems that affect them. Such an ethic recognizes that public speaking is an opportunity for public advocacy about the many ills that plague society, and that not realizing that ethic is, in a sense, an abdication of our responsibility to realize a world with less hunger, suffering, and injustice. For example, you could ask students

> **identity**
> the communicative performance associated with negotiating both ascribed (i.e., things people think, feel, or act like toward a perceived group) and avowed (i.e., things a person thinks, feels, or acts like based on their belief that they belong to a group) orientations
>
> **positionalities**
> the different positions (e.g., ablebodiedness, class, gender, race, or sexuality) that a person inhabits in society

to pick different parts of their *identity* and explore those *positionalities* (e.g., race, gender, or class) for an informative speech. Or, ask them to advocate on behalf of an oppressed community or counter to a community of privilege that they belong to in a persuasive speech. Public speaking assignments should encourage students to view themselves as simultaneously privileged and oppressed, adopting an intersectional focus. Public speaking should help students understand the cultural, historical, and material dimensions of inequality in connection to their lived experiences.

A second and often overlooked dimension of teaching public speaking is the relationship between speaker and audience. When audience analysis is taught, it usually focuses on how to be effective or efficient in a public speech event (e.g., how to craft a message to persuade a hostile or receptive audience). However, we believe that public speaking pedagogy is not simply concerned with teaching speakers how to find ways to impose their worldview onto different types of audience (see Foss & Griffin, 1995). Instead, we encourage students to view themselves as a part of the community that they are advocating *with*. Such a view engenders a different type of relationship between speaker and audience than a traditional view; that is, it encourages students to view public speaking as a process of negotiation with others in order to find solutions to the problems that face a community.

One way that you can cultivate this ethic in class is to share the power of grading with students during public speeches. If you are the only person with the power to grade a speech, then it runs the risk of teaching a hidden curriculum—that students should cater their speeches to the whims of the most powerful person in the room (in this case, you). If you plan to involve students in the grading process (and we hope you do), then you must teach students how to be ethical and discerning graders. Simply asking students to assign a number to their peers is not only dehumanizing to both parties, it does not make explicit the culture of power (see Chapter 3) in grading. Instead, work to generate an assessment tool with students so they are involved and knowledgeable about the process. Doing so not only helps students become knowledgeable about assessment practices within your class, it also helps humanize the process of public speaking.

As you develop assessment tools for public speaking, we believe there is an important caveat you should keep in mind: there is no such thing as an ideal public speaker or speech. With that important caveat in mind, we have provided a sample persuasive public speech rubric that you can use in your class (see Appendix B). Remember, you can always collaborate with students to adapt the rubric to better match your classroom culture and design. Although teaching students a traditional form of speech (e.g., introduction, body, and conclusion) is useful, it should not be viewed as the only way or necessarily even the best way to engage in a public speech. To act as if there is only one way to perform a good speech perpetuates a hidden curriculum—one that privileges White, male, and Eurocentric forms of expression. Demonstrate different types of public speeches through video examples or texts, and (just as important) encourage students to perform their speeches in those ways. Overall, teach students that a good speech, and a good speaker, is more than a mere formula—it is loving work done with others.

ESSAYS

In our experience, writing essays remains a ubiquitous practice within higher education. Instructors often use essays as a way to assess students' abilities to review specific material, synthesize various sources, and/or develop an argument (Cooper & Odell, 1971). Much like the public speech, we believe that assessment through essays should go beyond just the mechanics (e.g., grammar, style, or organization) to help students cultivate a critical engagement with texts. We do not mean to suggest that the mechanics of writing are unimportant; indeed, Freire (2000) advocates that critical instructors must teach students how to read the word (skill) and world (ethic) in order to transform society. Thus, essays should not be used to teach skills divorced from ethics nor to brow-beat students into mimicking social justice jargon back to the teacher (see Chapter 5); instead, they should be a place where students are free to develop both their skills as writers and their ethics as change agents. In this section, we offer two ways that you might use essays to enhance a critical communication pedagogical approach to classroom instruction.

One way encourage the use of essays as a form of critical assessment is to engage in progressive grading. In our experience, instructors all too often engage in the following practice when assigning essays: 1) the instructor assigns an essay for students to write; 2) students write an essay and turn it in; 3) the instructor grades it and hands it back; 4) students skip over the instructor's notes, look at the grade, and throw the paper away. Rarely do these instructors talk with students about feedback (other than when students try to challenge a grade). Instead, students are given an endless parade of grades and handwritten notes (some of which they can't read or understand) and are expected to learn how to write from this process.

We agree with critical scholars (e.g., Danielewicz & Elbow, 2009; Shor, 2009) that such practices disempower students because they do not provide ways for students to meaningfully explore their ideas while developing their writing skills. One way to engage in progressive grading is to provide feedback on a paper in chunks. For example, a student would turn in the first two pages of an essay, an instructor would provide feedback. The student would then make corrections and turn in the revised pages, as well as the next two pages of the essay, and the instructor would continue this process until the essay was complete. The grade for the essay would be based on the final product, which encourages the student to work through each round of feedback. By viewing the essay as a collaborative project over the course of the semester (rather than simply a display of knowledge), you can work with students to cultivate writing skills while also humanizing each other.

Peer editing is another way that students can learn writing skills while developing a critical ethic. Importantly, peer editing should not be viewed as simply an opportunity for students to catch each other's mistakes (or as a way to make your grading load easier). Rather, peer editing should be understood as a collaboration between two (or more) students in relation to their mutually assigned task. Such an ethic requires time and attention in order to cultivate. First, instructors should provide a self- or student-generated rubric and explain how students should utilize it. By providing a rubric and asking for them to look for a finite collection of rules, errors, or topics, you not only help them become a better peer reviewer, you also help them learn those rules for their own writing development. Second, instructors should give time for students to debrief each other about their feedback. By encouraging students to explain their reasons for their comments, you provide a chance for them to agree or disagree with each other's assessment and find ways to negotiate their difference of opinion. Overall, peer editing provides a space for students to see each other as experts and thus learn about and from one another.

Although essays can be a powerful tool to encourage collaboration, you will still be faced with the challenge of providing feedback. When offering comments to student work, give specific, legible, and substantive feedback. Saying "Paragraph is unclear" is much less helpful than "Provide a topic sentence for paragraph." Of course, if you are teaching students who do not know what a "topic sentence" is, then even this may not be concrete enough. One way to make sure your feedback is clear is to schedule student meetings during your office hours or in lieu of class time to go over feedback. This practice ensures that students have a clear understanding of your feedback, while also giving you the chance to understand your students and their learning needs. Additionally, you should prioritize feedback—do not just edit a student's paper! Try providing feedback in the following order: content, overall organization, paragraph construction, and grammar/spelling. Providing feedback on all of these dimensions is not only time prohibitive, it can become overwhelming to students when they try to address your comments.

Most importantly, do not view feedback as an obligation to "correct" students' writing—such a view perpetuates a hidden curriculum that "good writing" is a transcendental fact rather than the production of certain styles and traditions in a given historical moment. Your job, as a critical educator, is to teach about and through these traditions in order to reveal the hidden curriculum and challenge its assumed normalcy. At the end of this book, we have included an essay rubric (see Appendix C) for the communication analysis paper assignment we detail in the sample syllabus. Importantly, you should ensure that students do not view "good writing" as an abstract goal; rather, help them understand their essay as a situated practice guided by rules and norms of the scholarly genre. As such, they should recognize that there are many ways to write well, and each tradition is not wholly applicable to other genres of writing (e.g., scholarly, narrative, personal, or journalistic). We hope that by doing so, you provide a space for students to explore a variety of ways of representing their thoughts through writing, and thus become empowered to articulate their ideas about social-justice to their audience.

PORTFOLIOS

Portfolios can take a variety of forms and serve different functions (see Johnston, 2004). For some teachers, a portfolio functions as a collage of reflection, journaling, and coursework that is both a formative (i.e., ongoing) and summative (i.e., overall) assessment. For others, a portfolio is simply a collection of all the work done over the course of a semester that is turned in as the student's summative assessment. Although some instructors create portfolio assignments that strongly mirror the types of documents or style that are dominant in the corporate world, others encourage students to view the assignment as a chance for self-exploration and transformation. We believe that portfolio assignments should focus on students' reflexive development, rather than on the production of documents that simply demonstrate some preconceived notion of competence. To that end, we offer some ways that you may use portfolio assignments as assessment tools that highlight, rather than hide, the hidden curriculum of schooling.

One important component of portfolios is their ability to be a place where students cultivate a deep, holistic, and nuanced accounting of their lived experiences. Drawing upon Kahl (2013), we argue that portfolios should help students "(1) heighten awareness of hegemony in the classroom and in society, (2) identify avenues for praxis, and (3) take steps toward praxis" (p. 2617). To this end, we suggest that a portfolio assignment should be a component of formative and summative assessment as students engage in some type of community advocacy. Throughout this process, students (and the teacher) should utilize reflexive journaling to connect their personal experiences with the political, material, and cultural dimensions of activist work. By reflexive journaling, we mean that students do not simply write about their experiences on a given day, but instead attempt to connect how their classed, gendered, or racialized identities reflect and produce the cultural systems that surround them (Kahl, 2013). The portfolio provides insights into the ways that students understand and incorporate a social justice focus within their daily experiences, rather than simply being a demonstration of vocabulary learned by rote.

Although the dominant understanding of a portfolio assignment may privilege writing as its preferred method of expression, we encourage you to explore avenues of expression beyond this narrow view of textual representation. Important educational theorists have long extolled the importance of arts-based, exploratory education for fostering social justice and democratic practices (e.g., Dewey, 1916; Greene, 2009). Interpretive dances, performances or skits, vlogs or blogs, paintings, and sculptures are just a few of the things that students can engage in or produce that can be a site where they cultivate deep and ongoing relationships with course content and other individuals. We encourage you to explore a variety of ways that students can work to make connections between their lived experiences and course content.

When assessing portfolios, many instructors tend to focus on the product that is produced (as a demonstration of knowledge), rather than view it as an ongoing conversation between the student and the teacher. If you incorporate a portfolio project into your class, we suggest that you use it as both a formative and summative form of assessment to capture its full potential as a place where you and a student can engage in dialogue about social justice (see Chapter 6). As someone using the portfolio as a formative assessment, your role is to challenge, and be challenged by, the student through their engagement with the topics raised in class. Importantly, you are not an arbiter of wrong or right answers, but rather a co-facilitator in a joint task of discovery. When using the portfolio as a summative assessment, your role is to ascertain how students have (or have not) incorporated the course content into their own lives. As Lynch (2001) argues, one important component of critical assessment should be how "participants change the way in which they relate to each other and to themselves" (p. 366). In short, you should focus on how students have developed (or not) their understanding of self/other and institutional/cultural systems that shape and constrain the lived experiences of everyone.

CONCLUSION

In this chapter, we've utilized the idea of the hidden curriculum (Giroux & Penna, 1983) to imagine holistic, nuanced, and transformative understandings of assessment. We've developed some ways that public speeches, essays, and portfolios can be used to cultivate ethics of community advocacy, reflexivity, and praxis. As we close this chapter, we wish to address some concerns we have struggled with as young professionals that we believe you may face as well.

Although we have offered some avenues to creating more socially just forms of assessment in this text, we do not believe that you should simply use them uncritically. In other words, imposing a grading system on students (no matter how socially just the assignments might be) is inherently anti-democratic. Now, to be clear, we do not mean that every type of assignment can or even should be created solely by students. However, if instructors wish to encourage students to exercise their creative and democratic capabilities in the classroom, then they must offer ways for students to practice those habits. One way to engage in this type of teaching is to work with students to generate a class-wide or individualized learning contract (Shor, 2009). Students are expected to propose the amount and type of work they wish to produce in the class, the criteria by which they will be evaluated, and/or the grading system (e.g., points or pass/fail) to be used. Although your department may dictate some or all of these items to you, we believe that (when possible) instructors should incorporate student feedback into the class (see Chapter 7). Such a system works to resist the hidden curriculum that teachers are the only ones capable or worthy of assessing student work.

Another concern is the relationship between assessment and grading. At the end of the semester (if not sooner), you will most likely have to assign some grade to a student's assignment or overall performance. However, there are ways to resist the logics that guide the practice of assigning grades. Because U.S. testing culture is so focused on viewing grades as a reflection of one's knowledge, students are often afraid to try new forms of expression (e.g., poetry) or engage in new types of assignment (e.g., community activism) because of the risk of failure. As a result, students are taught a hidden curriculum that some modes of expression are "better" than others simply because they are the most used within institutions of higher education. One way to resist this ethic is to create a course contract that guarantees a B if certain minimum requirements are met. By guaranteeing a set grade for minimum expectations, students can be encouraged to try something that is new, difficult, or unfamiliar. Therefore, not only are students empowered as critically aware individuals, the implicit and dehumanizing link between grades and intelligence is subverted.

Probably most important to the discussion about critical assessment and the hidden curriculum is the reminder that instructors cannot grade students on their consciousness. As Shor (2009) articulates, "Lecturing or sermonizing at students will silence many and encourage others to mimic the teacher's bombast to win As for being so 'bright'" (pp. 20–21). Telling students how to think or feel and grading them on their ability to mimic the ideas or words you want simply trades one set of imposed ideas for another. Instead, your grading should reflect the development that students exhibit over the course of a semester. Their work should demonstrate that they are trying to make sense of the ideas and concepts that are discussed in class, rather than simply regurgitating them. We believe that if you work toward this ethic you will find that students produce work that is intellectually rigorous and daring.

Journal/Discussion Questions

1. What does an "ethic of reflection" in assessment mean to you?
2. As a student, how would you feel about being an equal partner in assessing yourself on a heavily weighted class project? In what ways would you struggle with this responsibility?
3. As a student, what assessment practices did you feel were unfair or completely out of your control? Why?
4. As a student, what assessment practices did you feel were fair or within your control? Why?
5. How much control do you think students should have over assignments? How much control do you think instructors should have over assignments? Why?
6. When assessing and providing feedback on speeches or essays, how will you react or grade personal or emotional disclosures (e.g., mental health, sexual violence, or racism)?

MENTORING AS AN ACT OF LOVE IN THE COMMUNICATION CLASSROOM

WE BELIEVE COMMUNICATION CREATES COMMUNITY. TO THIS EXTENT, WE ASK OURSELVES (AND BY EXTENSION, YOU): WHAT KIND OF COMMUNITY DO YOU WANT? WHAT KIND OF COMMUNITY WILL NURTURE AND SUSTAIN YOU? WHAT KINDS OF COMMUNITIES DO WE NEED FROM OUR CLASSROOMS? WHAT ROLE, WHAT RESPONSIBILITY DO YOU SHARE IN CREATING A COMMUNITY THAT IS NURTURING FOR OTHERS?

WARREN AND FASSETT (2011, P. 38)

I WALK INTO THE CLASSROOM. It's the second day of classes in the fall semester, so I'm not really familiar with the students yet. Most of them are already in their desks, talking to one another about the class they shared before this one. I set my book and class roster on the podium. The students are all laughing at a joke one of them just told. I stand awkwardly at the front, feeling a bit like the on-the-outs nerd I was in high school. Should I interrupt their conversation? I look at the clock and see it is a few minutes past 11:00. I don't want them to think I'm some power-hungry maniac who can just stop their conversation whenever I please, but class should have already started. Some students are looking at me expectantly. I smile back, hesitantly, and drop my gaze. With one more mental rehearsal of "I can do this," coursing through my head, I raise my head, clear my throat and, as if by magic, the students all look at me as one.

"Hey everyone," I say, a bit unnerved by their almost synchronous response. "I thought that maybe we could start off with an icebreaker to get to know each other better. Let's do one-minute introduction speeches. Just tell the class your name and a little bit about yourself. Does anyone want to go first?"

An African American female student raises her hand. "Yeah, go for it!" I say and start clapping. Other students join in the applause, the sound of it swelling as she reaches the front of the classroom. I walk to the back of the class and sit in an empty desk.

Josephine starts off simply enough. She greets the class, tells us her name, and what she wants to do after she completes college. Then she starts describing her experiences before enrolling college. As she recounts times when she faced abuse by her parents, racism at the hands of police officers, and hunger because her family couldn't afford food, she begins to break down and cry. Between her sobs, she articulates how getting a college degree will make sure she never has to endure the trauma she went through as a child.

Josephine's speech trails off and she stands at the front of class, weeping with her head down. I am simultaneously moved by her vulnerability and completely unprepared to respond to her speech. I thought students were just going to recount some hobbies! I sit in the desk, unsure about what I should do. Another African American female, Niqui, stands up out of her desk, walks to the front where Josephine is and hugs her. Josephine's head rests on the other student's shoulder as Niqui strokes Josephine's head and coos softly. Niqui looks at me, I nod, and she leads Josephine out of the class and into the hall. Again, almost as one, the students in class look back at me. I realize my mouth is open. I shut it with an audible *click*.

I'm torn between my perceived duties as an instructor and not wanting this moment—this real, beautiful, and terrible moment—to be swept away by the institutional concern to cover ground. "Okay," I stammer. "Well. Right, when we see Josephine next, let's make sure we thank her for her bravery." The students continue to stare at me. "Okay. Right. Well," I repeat, my face growing hot. "I guess if someone else wants to go, then we can continue." After a few moments of awkward silence, another student gets up and gives his speech. He spends most of his time talking about his cat. I don't know whether I should be relieved or sad as student after student recount a series of disconnected facts about their lives, listing off items that seem removed from any emotional investment.

****

As we think about the ways that teachers touch and are touched by the students in their lives, we reflect on how students and teachers can form loving relationships.

Central to this ethic is the notion that students and teachers must work to remedy the culture of disconnection that seeks to normalize vacuous and inauthentic interactions within and beyond the classroom. Love, in a critical sense, does not mean unreflective acceptance of others' worldviews or viewpoints. Think back on the relationships you have had with your family, friends, or romantic partners—have they always been free of disagreement or strife? Most likely, you have had frustrating, even angry, arguments with someone that you have loved. And, although you might need to walk away from the situation for minutes, hours, or even days, it is your love for the other person that leads you back to continue the conversation.

According to Freire (2000), a critical understanding of love encourages instructors to appreciate each moment of vulnerability as an act of courage, one that demands commitment on the part of the critical educator to work with their students to realize a better world. Kyle R.'s opening story shows how, even within this ethic, instructors can sometimes be caught off guard by the very thing we wish to cultivate. Educational systems are so ingrained with a value of neutrality, objectivity, and the "life of the mind" that it is sometimes hard to recognize that students are real, living, breathing people with stories, histories, and experiences. Cultivating loving relationships with students is an important component of resisting the routine, everyday ways that people are dehumanized within institutions that do not foreground love. As Freire (2000) states, "If I do not love the world—if I do not love life—if I do not love people—I cannot enter into a dialogue" (p. 90). In other words, social justice educators cannot just rely upon the insightfulness of their intellectual critiques, but must authentically and uncompromisingly love their students to fulfill their transformative potential.

We recognize that it may sound odd to say that you should love your students and believe that assertion beyond the sound bite of the loving teaching (complete with shiny red apple and ruler). As hooks (1994) observes, the notion that students and teachers can truly love one another is still very much viewed with contempt in academia. To love students necessitates investing in their lives, struggles, and ambitions, recognizing that sometimes your desires will come secondary to their needs, advocating with them even when it is politically and emotionally risky, and challenging them when they say or do things that perpetuate oppression. But, most of all, it means you never stop doing the heart work of teaching, because a society where people love each other—truly, honestly, and deeply love each other—can only be realized when those relationships are modeled in our everyday lives. In this chapter, we "reframe" seemingly mundane activities that are not viewed as part the "special labor" of mentoring—attendance policies, class participation, and office hours—as opportunities for cultivating a loving student-instructor relationship. Although there are certainly a wide range of ways to show and offer love, we address these three areas because they are common components of instructors' labor.

CLASS ATTENDANCE

We suspect that if you reflect back on the relationships in your life, you will find that being present for your family members, romantic partners, or other loved ones was an important component of fostering a loving relationship. One does not cultivate a loving relationship with another person without some expectation for (semi)regular interaction. To wit, a person cannot say, "I love you, but I never want to be around you." Such an assertion is simply laughable.

As instructors, we intuitively know that students who regularly attend class tend to perform better on assignments. That this commonsense notion is backed by research (e.g., Credé, Roch, & Kieszczynka, 2010; Gump, 2005) only adds weight to the notion that students should attend class. We believe the overall message is clear—students who attend class tend to perform better than those who do not. However, we also believe that how instructors craft and implement an attendance policy should go beyond pragmatic concerns and work toward creating a foundation for an ongoing, loving relationship.

If instructors think of their interactions with students as cultivating a loving relationship, then attendance policies take a renewed sense of purpose. We do not believe that a loving relationship is characterized by ticking off how many times one sees her or his significant other—love is not built on a quota system. Furthermore, students should not feel obligated to attend class simply to avoid punishment or to gain some reward. At the same time, we do think you should offer clear expectations (whether self- or student generated) for student attendance, in order to be explicit about the culture of power (see Chapter 3). Although certainly there are times when we feel obligated to be around significant others (we're looking at you, holidays!), obviously fostering relationships with others involves more than just our physical presence. To that end, we offer that to sustain your relationship with students, it is important that you show your investment in students' lived experiences.

Although certainly there are a range of ways that instructors can show they care about students, we offer two practices that we utilize in our classrooms.[1] First, students should feel invested in the classroom. Relationships are not healthy when only one person is invested in making it work. If you are making all of the decisions for the class, then it would be difficult (if not impossible) for students to feel as if they are valued members of the classroom. For example, if you were in a romantic relationship where your partner made all of the decisions (from where to eat to finances), then you would probably not feel like an equal. Asking for and implementing student input about classroom policies, course texts, and course management are important ways to cultivate a loving relationship with students. In other words, give students a reason to show up to class other than avoiding punishments associated with poor attendance.

Second, you should take the time to learn about and mentor your students. This practice starts on day one when you begin to learn students' names and dispositions through structured activities and icebreakers (see Chapter 8), and continues throughout and beyond the semester. Listening to your students is perhaps one of the most powerful components of this ethic. Many students struggle with family, health, relationship, financial, and mental-health issues while enrolled in higher education. As a loving instructor, you must create a classroom culture where they feel open to talk with you (and, hopefully, others) about these issues. One way to encourage this type of environment is to email students when they have missed multiple days of class, to talk with them about their class attendance. Ask them why they have missed class, not as a way to ascertain if their excuse is good enough or not, but to open conversations about the issues that face them. Although some instructors may feel that this practice is too much like babysitting students, we argue that (when viewed through a lens of love) regular contact with students provides an important function—it lets them know that someone sees and cares about them. In our experience, instructors who think they are too smart, important, or busy to keep in contact with students get out of their relationships exactly what they put into them: nothing.

---

1   We want to be clear—these are not empty strategies that we employ with students to give the semblance of care. An important component of a loving relationship is honesty, and we do not believe that instructors should be artificial in their interactions with students.

When classroom attendance is viewed through an ethic of love, it reframes conversations about our obligations to ourselves and our students. Although the practices we offer do not ensure that you will never have attendance problems in your classes, we do believe that they have the potential to act as a catalyzing force for student investment in the classroom. As you begin or continue your teaching career, remember the instructor or teacher who was your most formative mentor. Were they simply a really smart person? Or, was their content knowledge made meaningful to you because of their desire to form a relationship with you? We suspect that their influence on your life was primarily due to how they interacted with you—the love they showed you over the course of a semester or many years. Keep that image, and that love, in your heart as you go into your class each day. We guarantee that many of your students will reciprocate that feeling if you give them the opportunity to do so.

CLASSROOM PARTICIPATION

Instructors want students to engage with the material they have provided for any given class session, resulting in one of the largest questions of the new (and seasoned) instructor: How can I get my students to read or talk? Although we certainly want our students to engage in classroom activities, we offer that this type of question implicitly defines students as passive receivers of instructors' desires. If instructors view their relationships with students as built upon an ethic of love, then they must see students as self-determining subjects with their own desires, hopes, and fears. A loving understanding of classroom participation therefore encourages instructors to view it as a way to open conversations, rather than simply a platform for students to demonstrate content knowledge. With this exhortation in mind, we offer ways that you may use classroom participation to foster loving relationships in the classroom.

Fostering loving relationships with and among students in the communication classroom means you must negotiate between the *dialectics* of structure and spontaneity. On one hand, your classroom must have some semblance of order. Most students will expect you to provide discussion questions, give lectures, and offer advice. These expectations require preparation on your part; you cannot just improvise for every class meeting. On the other hand, being overly

dialectics
two simultaneously true, yet mutually exclusive, categories

structured will bar some students from exploring avenues of investigation that help them make sense of their lived experiences. Being overly structured ensures that classroom discussion centers on topics that are of interest to *you*. Although there will certainly be times when your and your students' interests will converge, the process of that mutual recognition should be negotiated rather than imposed. Classroom participation should not be wholly dictated by you or by the students—such dynamics would either be too authoritarian or lackadaisical. Rather, classroom participation should emerge as a result of a continued appreciation of and engagement among the instructor, students, and course texts.

If you plan on assessing classroom participation, then it is important that you provide multiple avenues for students to display their engagement with each other or the course texts. For example, awarding participation points to students who verbally contribute to class discussion privileges speaking as the only form of authentic engagement. Furthermore, demands for verbal contributions can alienate students whose cultural orientation places emphasis on quiet deliberation, who self-identify as introverted, or who fear their contribution may be viewed negatively by other members in the classroom (see Hao, 2011). In addition to verbal contributions, instructors should provide ways for students to provide written, video, or aesthetic contributions (see Chapter 8 for examples). In our experience, simply forcing students to demonstrate content knowledge on a multiple-choice pop quiz is not a sufficient motivator for students to become connected to the classroom culture. Sticks and carrots usually motivate only those students who are grade rather than learning oriented, and tend to harm the quality of students' thinking (Kohn, 2011). As an instructor, you should not search for a magic bullet to elicit participation from students. Such a view dehumanizes students into passive receivers of your will. Instead, participation should be viewed as a way to encourage you and your students to jointly identify and explore the problems that face them and you.

Classroom participation, when viewed as a component of a loving relationship, is more than just a way to simply monitor students' progress or gauge their study habits. Rather, it provides opportunities for students and instructors to explore ideas together. Even when used as a form of assessment, classroom participation can be a powerful way to start and continue conversations about topics within and beyond the classroom. In our experience, many students are more inclined to participate when they see you reciprocate the nature and depth of their contributions. By being open and honest with students, you set the ground work for a relationship based on trust and empathy. We can think of no better foundation for a loving relationship.

OFFICE HOURS

A common lament among instructors—from graduate-student teachers to full professors—is that undergraduate students do not visit during office hours. Of course, not every instructor wants to converse with students during office hours. In fact, we have interacted with professors who have actively discouraged us from seeking their help or insight outside of class. We hope that you will not be (or are not) this type of instructor. Although certainly your office hours can be used to get caught up on grading, craft research, or answer emails, we believe that it is first and foremost an important space for students and instructors to interact with one another and grow together. In this section, we first explore some reasons why students might not take advantage of office hours before then explaining some ways to encourage relationship building through structured conversation.

When considering the reasons why students may not attend office hours, we think it is helpful to think about their lived experiences both before and after enrolling in college. Many undergraduate students' mental frameworks for thinking about office hours are shaped by their time in K–12 schooling. For many students, having to speak with an instructor one-on-one probably signals one of two things: 1) the student is in trouble, or 2) the student is struggling with the course material. Neither of these are exciting or positive reasons for visiting an instructor.

Undergraduate students, particularly first-year and sophomore students, may not understand that office hours can be an opportunity to develop a relationship with an instructor. Even junior and senior students may not see the positive aspects of office hours if they have not had interactions with college instructors that challenge their preconceived notions about the function of office hours. Another reason students may not visit office hours is because they may think of them as a way to elicit information from an instructor (e.g., ask about material missed due to an absence). If students think of office hours in a purely functional spirit, then they may be inclined to simply send an email to an instructor rather than physically show up to office hours. Finally, office hours may conflict with students' other classes or work schedules. In our experience, students will often pick their work, school, or family obligations over what they perceive as superfluous time spent in an instructor's office.

It is important to note that some students may simply not want to cultivate a relationship with an instructor. Perhaps the student's and your personality do not match well. There is, of course, no reason why every student has to (or even could) like every instructor. Instructors have their own personalities and quirks, and students may not appreciate them (and vice versa). Students may also dislike their instructors who critique the systems that sustain privilege that the students benefit from in their life. In these instances, students may not want to engage in discussions that they feel might make them uncomfortable about their own identity, and so they forego office hour conversations. Overall, it is important to realize that these reasons (as well as others) play a role in students' decision to (not) attend office hours. Simply labeling students as too lazy to attend office hours is not only hopelessly simplistic, it defines students' identities while conveniently eliding the role instructors can play in encouraging authentic conversations.

In order to encourage students to develop a relationship with you, we suggest that you redefine the purpose of holding office hours at the beginning of the semester. Rather than viewing office hours primarily as an obligation or fact-giving event, we suggest that they can be time to engage in structured conversations with students about the issues that they and you face, uniquely and jointly. The important component of this ethic is the word "structured." Simply saying, "My office door is always open" does not address many of the reasons that students do not attend office hours in the first place. To show students the transformative potential that office hour conversations can have, you must invest your time and energy into making sure they are worth students' time.

One way to achieve this aim is to make office hours a required component of each class you teach. If you teach classes with small enrollment, then meeting students one-on-one at least once during the semester can be a great way start learning about one another. Students can ask content-related questions if they want, but do not have to feel a sense of shame associated with requesting what they may perceive to be extra or remedial time. Instead, you have provided a forum for them to air their classroom concerns, which also gives you opportunities to explore extracurricular subjects (e.g., family, hobbies, or ambitions). If you are teaching a large lecture class, then ask students to form groups of three to five and then make the appointments for office hours. Although less personalized, such a tactic gives students the chance to interact with you in a more informal way. For large or small enrollment classes, you may also set aside a few days over the semester to meet students during the regularly held class time. Overall, making an explicit attempt to incorporate out-of-class interactions may encourage students to be more inclined to come during your regular office hours in the future to talk with you. In order to meet with all of the students in your class, you may have to meet them outside of your regular office hours. Certainly, you should take care of yourself and never overcommit yourself. At the same time, we have found that investing our time and attention is the best way to create meaningful, authentic, and equitable relationships with students.

Overall, office hours can provide a great avenue for cultivating understanding and collaboration between and among students and instructors. Once you show students that your commitment to their lives goes beyond simply being in your office at a predetermined time, you will find that they will regularly come to you for advice or support about issues beyond your class content. Although you are certainly not a therapist, you may find that you will provide many of the same functions—a shoulder to lean (or cry) on. Share in each other's triumphs and failures, and work toward creating a foundation of mutual respect and love. You will be surprised by how rewarding students, and you, will find it.

CONCLUSION

In this chapter, we have discussed the importance of creating and maintaining relationships with students. We offered that such a practice must be predicated upon an ethic of love—a deep and authentic care for students' lived experiences. We argued that by redefining attendance, participation, and office hours as practices of a loving relationship, you could work toward modeling relationships that are grounded in social justice. Although there is no way to ensure that every student will like you (and vice versa), we believe that working toward an ethic of love in the classroom challenges instructors to be better to themselves and others.

Importantly, you should remember that you should strive for a mentoring relationship rather than one of friendship. Although certainly you may become friends after a semester is over or even be friendly with students, there are clear institutional and cultural logics that shape and constrain the relationship (see Rudick & Golsan,

2014). The fact that you will hold a position of institutional authority and power cannot be dismissed. To overlook the ways that students and instructors marshal and exercise power differently within the college classroom goes beyond mere naïveté and begins to mimic the denial of power by members of privileged groups. We believe your relationships with students will be harmed more by your futile disavowal of power than its recognition and negotiation. A loving relationship requires trust—and trust is only gained by being honest and open with students about the dynamics of your relationship over the course of the semester or following years.

Journal/Discussion Questions

1. What components of a loving mentorship were vital to you as a student? Do you try to model these components for your students or peers?
2. As a mentor, how do you envision yourself committing to a social justice relationship with your students?
3. In what ways will you try to practice self-care against emotionally draining relationships with students? With your peers? With your faculty?
4. In what ways will you allow yourself to be mentored and cared for by your students? Your peers? Your faculty?
5. What does a caring, mindful mentoring instructor look like to you? Does this image work for those different from you?

CRITICAL DIALOGUE AND PITFALLS IN THE COMMUNICATION CLASSROOM

IF THE CLASSROOM IS A MICROCOSM OF WORLDS, A METONYM OF THE CULTURES WE'LL ENCOUNTER THROUGHOUT OUR LIVES, THEN IT IS ALSO A SITE OF SOCIAL CHANGE. IT IS A MEANINGFUL ENVIRONMENT FOR ENGAGING DIFFERENCE, FOR CREATING COMMUNITY, AND FOR ENVISIONING THE KINDS OF SOCIAL ORGANIZATION WE WANT FOR OURSELVES.

FASSETT AND WARREN (2007, P. 63)

THE 16-PASSENGER VAN, PAINTED GREEN WITH A WHITE NORTHEASTERN STATE UNIVERSITY LOGO, ROCKS BACK AND FORTH AS WE SPEED DOWN THE HIGHWAY TOWARD SALINA, KANSAS. The eight people in the van are listening to music, sleeping, or reading, trying to relax a little bit before we begin our performances at the speech and debate tournament at Kansas Wesleyan University the next day. As is often the case, I sit in the passenger seat in the front. Dr. Amy Aldridge Sanford, our team's coach, wants someone to talk with to keep her from getting drowsy while driving the long distances, and I happily oblige. I enjoy talking with her about communication philosophy, debate theory, and other issues that my friends and parents don't find interesting. This time, we settle on a discussion about the Miss NSU pageant and the Miss Black NSU pageants.

"Did you see the article in the student newspaper about the Miss Black NSU pageant they are starting this year?" Amy asks.

"Yeah, I read the opinions from the students on campus too. They are not happy with having a separate pageant." I reply, thinking about the deluge of opinions railing against the new show.

"Yeah," Amy said, rolling her eyes, "White students certainly seem upset about not getting to control another organization on campus. Did you read the response Dion wrote defending the Miss Black NSU pageant?"

"Yeah, but I didn't agree with it." I say, completely missing her nonverbal signals or the way she subtlety corrected me for saying "students" when I was really only referring to White students' outrage. "I mean, it's like they want to compete in both Miss NSU and Miss Black NSU. It just doesn't seem fair."

"Do you think so? You don't think there's a problem that there's never been an African American female win?" Amy asks.

"Yeah, it's a problem, but that doesn't mean they should get to have two chances. It's not fair. It's like the Black Entertainment Television network. Black actors get to be in normal shows and in Black shows, but there's nothing for just White people. Like, if I created a White Entertainment Television station then I'd probably be called a racist." I say, in a triumphant bit of logic that has impressed my other White peers in the past.

"Kyle, there is a White Entertainment Television." Amy says, giving me a side-eye.

"Yeah? Really?"

"Yeah, really. It's the 999 channels that aren't the BET."

****

A persistent theme in our writing is that the world is "rife with contradictions and asymmetries of power and privilege" (McLaren, 2002, p. 193). However, you may wonder, "If inequality is so bad, then why don't people just rise up and stop it?" This is a good question, and one that critical scholars have devoted a lot of time and attention to exploring. Perhaps the most influential writer on this subject is Antonio Gramsci, an Italian scholar who was imprisoned by the fascist Italian government during World War II. Gramsci argued that people are born into a set of historical, economic, and cultural systems, and raised within those systems to believe that they are normal, neutral, and natural. When people believe a system is common sense or unalterable, he referred to it as *hegemony*. Kyle R.'s experience shows how he used to believe that race-neutral strategies were

> **hegemony**
> The process by which meaning is structured to maintain dominant interests.

the most effective method of ensuring fairness, even though it was obvious that supposedly unbiased books, television shows, movies, and beauty pageants were overwhelmingly White. Those van rides, and Amy's wise words, were probably the most formative moments in his development as a social justice advocate and communication scholar. They made the invisible visible by challenging his previously held assumptions about the normalcy of inequality.

Kyle R.'s experience is not unique. Students have often internalized the realities of status quo as normal or common sense, and are sometimes resistant to the idea that things should (or even can) be changed. Certainly, some students will enter your classes with a strong belief in social justice and may be well-versed in various forms of activism. However, our experiences lead us to believe that the majority of your students will espouse a variety of hegemonic beliefs. For example, some students may believe that inequality exists, but that only minor reforms are needed to correct a largely fair society, whereas others may assert that inequality is a natural result of individual work ethic.

One the most daunting and challenging parts of being a social justice educator is engaging in dialogue with students in order to have sensitive and thorough conversations about systems of privilege and oppression. Kyle R., for example, felt ashamed when Amy's words challenged him to understand his privileged position in front of the other members of the team on the bus. However, doing so encouraged him to stop arguing and reflect on the implications of Amy's words. Of course, Amy's tactic is not a magic bullet that will work in every instance or for every student. How you introduce and conduct discussions about privilege and oppression will have to be reflective of the relationships you have built (or not) with students before you can ask them to challenge their hegemonic beliefs. Additionally, you can't always guarantee that students who are strongly located in privileged groups will be quick to change. Kyle C., for instance, had a variety of conversations with his debate coaches about similar issues, but it took a many years of self-reflection and engagement with theories of social justice before he was able to recognize that racism was something that occurred within structures of power, and not only in individual actions or decisions.

In this chapter, we will explore some of the pitfalls that instructors and students will experience while they seek to engage in dialogic communication (see Hytten & Warren, 2004; Warren & Hytten, 2004). We synthesize literature about common responses that we, and other social justice educators, have encountered in our classes when attempting to engage in dialogue with students. We hope that by doing so, you can identify and learn from some of our mistakes in your own journey to be a social justice educator.

PITFALLS TO CRITICAL DIALOGUE

THE PITFALL OF HEGEMONIC CIVILITY

In our years of teaching, we have seen male students talk over female students when the latter try to discuss issues of feminism or gender discrimination, White students who have left the room in the middle of Black students' persuasive speeches on issues of racism, and cisgender students who have simply remained silent and disengaged when trans students discussed issues of anti-trans violence. Although we are now better at recognizing and engaging with these dynamics, we remember and regret the times when we didn't intervene quickly or forcibly enough because we did not want to be viewed as an authoritarian instructor. This desire to maintain cordial relationships more than challenge inequality is a form of hegemonic civility, and a pitfall to dialogue (Patton, 2004).

You certainly do not want to cultivate a class where people are routinely uncivil to each other. An important component of creating a classroom climate where students feel comfortable expressing their views comes with the knowledge that they will not be silenced, ridiculed, or emotionally harmed. At the same time, we have seen instances where students' and instructors' desire for civility has overridden their commitment to social justice. They create a classroom environment where people are too comfortable—where their hegemonic beliefs about privilege and oppression are not adequately challenged.

Hegemonic civility is particularly pernicious because it makes what seems to be a very rational appeal to be "nice" or "polite" while undermining conversations about social justice issues. For example, we have had White students who have said that they do not like talking about race because it makes them uncomfortable to listen to students of color speak about their experiences of racism. These students often claim that they feel attacked when discussing White privilege and racism. We find appeals like this often mask White students' fear—fear of responsibility, fear of people of color, and fear of giving up the control they have due to their privilege. They often attempt to enforce hegemonic civility through tone shaming, such as asserting that people of color are too loud, angry, or confrontational when they talk about racism. White students who appeal to hegemonic civility engage in what DiAngelo (2011) labels a "white fragility" or "a state in which even a minimum amount of racial stress becomes intolerable, triggering a range of defensive moves" (p. 57). By engaging in hegemonic civility, they are able to avoid talking about the issue at hand (i.e., racism and White supremacy) by critiquing the tone, language, or emotion of students of color. Such appeals function to maintain cordial relationships for privileged people at the experience of deep and meaningful engagement with social justice topics.

To cultivate an ethic of critical dialogue, you must find ways to break through hegemonic civility by showing privileged students that conversations about social justice are often emotionally difficult. For example, when we teach about racism, we have had success showing parts or all of the film *The Color of Fear*, which shows a racially diverse cast of men discuss racism in the United States. There are times when the men of color try to convince a White male that racism exists through very calm argumentation (i.e., offering statistics and personal testimonies) and other times when they become agitated. As such, the film demonstrates the need to bring all types of expression to bear when dialoguing about injustice, and the importance of speaking from the heart when discussing lived experiences. Another strategy to break down hegemonic civility is to encourage students to reflexively journal about their experiences over the course of the semester to explore how they talk to others concerning issues of privilege and oppression. And, if they don't have those conversations in their normal activities, to detail their fears and frustrations that inhibit them from engaging in dialogic conversation. Such work encourages them to be reflexive within their interactions and to be accountable to the ways that power shapes their desires or abilities to explore social justice issues.

Overall, hegemonic civility "favors those already in positions of power because those who wish to alter the status quo must regulate and mediate their speech to satisfy the powerful" (Simpson, 2008, p. 152). In other words, hegemonic civility limits the ways that oppressed people can express themselves about privilege and oppression. As a result, it ensures that discussion about social justice topics always caters to the imaginations of privileged people. Remind students that authentic relationships among people are not characterized by the absence of conflict, but by the ways that those encounters are interpreted and acted upon—in fact, often, conflict is the only route to change. If students and teachers wish to engage in dialogue, and challenge oppression, then learning from their mistakes and committing to doing better is the only way to build communities of love.

THE PITFALL OF HEGEMONIC RESISTANCE

Communication and education scholars often discuss student resistance as a classroom management issue that has its roots in instructors' lack of ability to direct student learning and engagement (see Burroughs, 2007). This literature is often predicated upon the assumption that the instructor–student partnership is essentially a superior–subordinate relationship, and places students as the recipients of instructors' will. Students who do not comply with instructors or "misbehave" engage in a range of behaviors to resist conforming to the instructors' desires. Although it is certainly important to think about how to best direct student learning, we depart from most literature in that we do not locate the source of students' opposition in their refusal to follow the instructor's commands. In fact, we encourage students to question our authority and explore avenues to create meaning for themselves. Rather, we locate student resistance in the adherence to hegemony and the refusal to recognize the validity of non-dominant ways of thinking. In this section, we talk about hegemonic resistance as those times when students try to physically intimidate or verbally abuse other students or the instructor to coerce them into silence about social justice.

To some, the need to challenge hegemonic civility while protecting yourself from hegemonic resistance might be a thin line to navigate. It is important that you recognize that students' disagreement, however vocal or angry, does not automatically constitute hegemonic resistance. For example, Kathryn taught a class composed primarily of first-generation students, and asked them to form groups and participate in a communication scavenger hunt for places on campus. She felt that doing so would help them bond with one another while offering them opportunities to find important places on campus and talk with campus officials. At the end of the activity, she awarded 10 bonus points to the team that found the most places. After the activity was over, a Latina student interrupted Kathryn, who was praising the first-place team, to ask why only one group received the points when everyone had fully participated in the activity. Kathryn, standing in front of the class, was caught off guard, and remembers having to forcibly remind herself not to simply react to what felt like a critique of her instruction and fall back on a "those were the rules" authoritarianism. As she listened to the Latina student, Kathryn recognized that her student was right and that this moment was exactly what she had been hoping to see—students advocating for themselves and valuing each other over the title of first place in the game. Admitting to the Latina student that she had a valid critique, Kathryn immediately amended the assignment rules. Ever since that time, Kathryn has always given the bonus points to all the students who find a minimum number of areas and recounts why she doesn't make the game a competition to each new class.

Instructors, particularly those from dominant positions, may find themselves uncomfortable when their students challenge their authority in the classroom. However, we have found that when we strive to build honest and caring relationships with students in the classroom, we are better able to differentiate between times when we are uncomfortable and when students make us (or others) feel threatened. Important to our understanding of this dynamic is the notion that students actively attempt to suppress conversations that challenge hegemonic thinking. For example, there was once a White male student in Kyle R.'s class who would often vocally disparage course materials, organization, and topics while in the middle of class discussion. After a day spent discussing racism in U.S. society, the student stayed after class to argue with Kyle about how White people are more oppressed than people of color. The student became angry during the exchange and accused him of being biased against White people—a funny proposition given Kyle's racial identification as a White person. As the White male student walked out the classroom door, he "casually" let him know that he liked the color of Kyle's home—yellow with green trim—and wondered aloud that it would be a shame if someone were to deface it. Kyle felt the students' not-so-subtle insinuation that he knew where Kyle lived constituted a threat to his safety. Although the student did not engage in physical violence, his response was clearly meant to suppress Kyle's willingness to continue working with the class to identify and challenge oppression. As an instructor, particularly if you identify with non-dominant groups or advocate for social justice in your classes, you may face similar situations.

The ways that students engage in hegemonic resistance can vary greatly. Sometimes students from marginalized identities will engage in *horizontal violence* by trying to shame, humiliate, or provoke members of their same

horizontal violence
harm, whether physical, mental, or symbolic, done by a member of a marginalized community to another member of that community

vertical violence

harm, whether physical, mental, or symbolic, done by a member of a dominant community to a member of a marginalized community

identity group. For example, students may embarrass each other for not acting White, straight, masculine, or middle class enough (or acting those positions too well). Other times, students from privileged identities will engage in *vertical violence*, directing abuse toward those who occupy marginalized identities in society. In those cases, it is important for you to remind students that the power of dialogue lies in people listening to one another and working together to investigate the underlying hegemonic beliefs that characterize oppressive opinions.

Sometimes these forms of violence are conducted by students with the best intentions. In Kyle C.'s classroom, students who have experience with sharing their voices quickly and easily will dominate discussion—based not in malice, but in an honest desire to share their thoughts and opinions. But, because we exist in a culture that encourages certain kinds of students to share their opinions, while dis-incentivizing others, Kyle C. sometimes has to ask these students to remember to leave space for the students who take more time to deliberate before sharing their thoughts. As Freire (1994) admonishes, although instructors do not have a right to be authoritarian, they have an obligation to use their authority on behalf of marginalized people. You may need to intervene into situations between students and exercise your authority by asking a student to leave the classroom, meet after class, or to be silent. Although openly displaying your power as an instructor may make you uncomfortable, we believe a greater harm is done to marginalized students by allowing hegemonic resistance to go unchallenged in the class.

Dialogue, as an ethic predicated upon mutual love, cannot be one sided. Such a view constitutes an abusive relationship where one party is supposed to defer to the wishes of the dominant party. Likewise, there is no place for instructors or students to engage in dialogue with students who purposively engage in hegemonic resistance and do not seek to change their behaviors. There is never a time when you should feel that you or other students deserve being abused or threatened while discussing course materials, nor is there need to romanticize those situations and "tough it out." Attempt to leave the situation and contact your supervisor as soon as possible. If you do not feel satisfied with the level of support you receive within your department, you may need to contact the graduate college on your campus.

THE PITFALL OF HEGEMONIC VERBALISM/ACTIVISM

In this section, we draw upon the work of Freire (2000), who differentiates between hegemonic verbalism and activism. On one hand, instructors and students who engage in hegemonic verbalism privilege talk without any intention of acting upon the knowledge they have built. In this ethic, critical communication pedagogy becomes just another theory that students have to learn, but do not have to experience or incorporate into their lives. On the other hand, hegemonic activism occurs when instructors and students act as if action, any action, is better than "simply" talking about oppression (Warren & Hytten, 2004). This type of ethic produces projects that identify needs within a community and propose or even enact solutions with little or no community input. At best, these projects fill immediate needs within the community (e.g., volunteering at a soup kitchen). At worst, they provide college students and instructors the opportunity to feel good about themselves and pad their résumé while harming, excluding, and further marginalizing the people they purport to serve. In either case, hegemony is left unchallenged by virtue of either inaction (i.e., hegemonic verbalism) or by maintaining hierarchies between those who have and those who need (i.e., hegemonic activism) when instructors and students encounter this pitfall.

Dialogic activism combines both verbalism and activism to create praxis. In other words, instructors and students are expected to remain in constant communication with each other, and the people they are purport to serve, to enact positive change within a community. Importantly, dialogic activism is predicated on the assumption that people within marginalized communities are the most knowledgeable about their needs and can best articulate the solutions that respect their histories. We are not advocating that every course that you teach must have a project that students engage in outside of class. Such an ethic views those outside of the walls of academia as means to an end (i.e., their problems become simply pedagogical tools). Rather, we suggest that you teach through an ethic emphasizing that teaching for social justice cannot just be done *about* marginalized populations, but must *with* and *for* them (Frey, Pearce, Pollock, Artz, & Murphy, 1996). In other words, it is not enough to recognize difference; you should intentionally and explicitly encourage students to take their knowledge, skills, and experiences and put them in service of people within marginalized communities. Listening to, and acting upon, the knowledge of marginalized people is the best way to ensure that instructors and students do not reinforce oppressive conditions in their struggle to identify and eliminate inequality.

As you teach your course, look for ways to incorporate dialogic activism within your class. Central to this task is recognizing that any need—poverty, hunger, or illness—is a systemic inequality rather than a matter of a person's individual worth or simply a need to be filled. The old saying, "Give a person a fish and they eat for a day. Teach a person to fish and they can eat for a lifetime" is particularly helpful here. The saying is a bit of hegemonic common sense: giving something to someone always and immediately makes them a dependent and we should strive to change people's attitudes, beliefs, or behaviors to fix inequality. However, we argue that sometimes a person needs a fish—immediate and temporary relief from oppressive circumstances. Other times, a person may need to learn to fish—to understand how to navigate systems to provide for themselves. However, a critical tradition should prompt you to explore two important questions: 1) Why did the person not know how to fish in the first place? and 2) What if there are no fish in the pond? These two questions call on us to explore how inequality is more than just a matter of changing individuals' circumstances, attitudes, or behaviors, and demands that we explore and change the structural reasons for oppression.

As you try to resist hegemonic verbalism/activism and strive for dialogic activism, we encourage you to continue to explore the ways that other scholars have addressed these issues. The most complete work to articulate what dialogic activism looks like within the communication studies discipline is Frey and Palmer's (2014) *Teaching Communication Activism*. This text provides a strong theoretical, conceptual, and pedagogical framework for going beyond mere charity and truly challenging ourselves and those around us to ground our advocacy in the voices of marginalized people. Furthermore, Chapter 8 of this text provides teaching activities that you can use to help you articulate how to work toward building dialogic relationships among students, and between your class and the community.

THE PITFALL OF HEGEMONIC SERMONIZING

Most traditional forms of pedagogy admonish against telling students your feelings or thoughts on important matters, such as religion or politics. Whereas traditional pedagogy stresses that teachers should be objective, we argue that objectivity is not possible and acting as if course materials, content, or organization are neutral is a mystification of hegemony. Critical and feminist scholars have shown time and again that dominant forms of knowledge represent the interests of privileged people, downplaying both the suffering and contributions of marginalized people (hooks, 1994; Zinn, 2001). More concretely, you will most likely require students to write essays, give speeches, or answer questions about issues that are inherently political (e.g., racism). To ask students to divulge sensitive information about themselves, but refuse to do so yourself, is an abuse of your power as the instructor. In short, we ask you to be open with your students and engage in reflexive dialogue with them about the issues that they face.

Although we believe you should reciprocate the level of disclosure you ask of students, we caution you against falling into the pitfall of hegemonic sermonizing. This ethic is characterized by the belief that your expert knowledge as an instructor (e.g., how to make a speech) gives you the moral authority to simply tell students how to act, feel, or believe. Freire (2000) labeled this communicative ethic the "banking model of education": students are expected to internalize and recite information given to them by an instructor. Importantly, hegemonic sermonizing can occur whether you are telling students how to think about the best ways to organize a speech or the best way to organize protests against sexual violence on campus. In other words, even if the content of your sermon is about social justice, you can still run into the pitfall because you are not allowing students to make meaning for themselves in regard to privilege and oppression. Any time you impose meaning on students, no matter how well intentioned, it is an act of cultural violence.

While at conferences about teaching and instruction, we often hear others who believe that Freire's (2000) caution against banking education is an indictment against all forms of lecture in the classroom. Although we applaud people who manage to never lecture, we believe that Freire's notion of banking goes beyond a simple lecture versus discussion dualism. For example, if there are times when instructors believe that students need course content delivered in a quick and efficient manner, and simply telling students that material is the best way to achieve that goal, is this a form of banking? Similarly, if an instructor relies entirely upon a question/discussion format, but only acknowledges or rewards students who give the answers that the instructor is looking for, is that dialogic?

We believe Freire's work challenges instructors to reflexively examine the ways that they interact with students and understand how their communication with them serves their *humanization* or *alienation*. We argue that it is not the mode of delivery that dictates whether an instructor is engaged in hegemonic sermonizing; rather, it is when instructors treat students as if they are objects that a banking education is realized. We encourage you to explain to students why you make the choices you do within the classroom (e.g., lecture, discussion, activity) and ask for student input about the best way to achieve course goals (which includes sometimes implementing their alternatives!). At Southern Illinois University, for example, teachers are asked to conduct a small-group instructional diagnosis of their class every semester, gathering qualitative data about how students are experiencing their classroom community. Though Kyle C. no longer teaches at SIU, in the middle of every semester he asks his students about the classroom community, through a short anonymous survey, by requiring students to write five to six sentences about what they like and dislike about the course content or method of instruction, what changes Kyle can make to help them in their learning process, and what changes students can make to create a better learning environment.

humanization

the process of realizing oneself as more fully human through relationships, empathy, and love

alienation

a state of feeling isolated, disconnected, or estranged from a sense of self and/or others

Critical communication pedagogy, as a social justice perspective grounded in the elimination of oppression, is unabashedly biased—against hunger, disease, suffering, and want. As the world lurches from one ecological, economic, and political disaster to the next, we remain convinced that there is no virtue in remaining detached, objective, or neutral. However, the belief that the world can and should be better should always be tempered by the dialogical ethic of articulating that reality *with each other*. Trampling on others in the quest to be right or to show yourself as the best social justice advocate trades love for animosity and collaboration for competition. We believe that being open with students is the best step toward engaging in dialogue and challenging oppression.

CONCLUSION

Dialogue is an important component of any social justice project. Not only does it provide an ethic for people to come together, name systems of oppression, and challenge hegemony, it exhorts them to humanize each other through this process. There is never a time when the goals of social justice outweigh the people engaged in advocacy—such a view treats people as mere instruments in service of revolutionary goals. Instead, you should strive to engage in sensitive and thorough inquiry with your students and jointly discover ways to make your communities hopeful, joyous, just, and loving places.

As you continue on your journey, keep in mind the pitfalls that we have outlined here. All-too-often we see insightful and hard-working social justice advocates fall into these traps and harm others in their mission to realize a just society. We too have to continue to be vigilant about how our advocacy can turn to arrogance. Although there will be times when you stumble and fall on your road to critical communication pedagogy, if you work to build loving relationships with students, we believe you will find a network of people who will support you and help you back on your journey. And, when they fall, you should do the same for them. When we reach out to others, either to offer or receive help, we acknowledge our own fallibility and build a system where we all realize a socially just world together.

Journal/Discussion Questions

1. What fears do you have when attempting to open dialogue about different social justice issues/topics with students?
2. Are there topics of social justice that make you more uncomfortable to dialogue about? Less uncomfortable? Why?
3. How do you respond to criticism of your work? Who does this type of response benefit or harm?
4. Does your response affect your ability to mindfully listen to that criticism?
5. What information about yourself do you feel might be too sensitive for you to share with your students? Why?
6. What types of questions do you find are the most helpful when attempting to open dialogue in class? Explain.

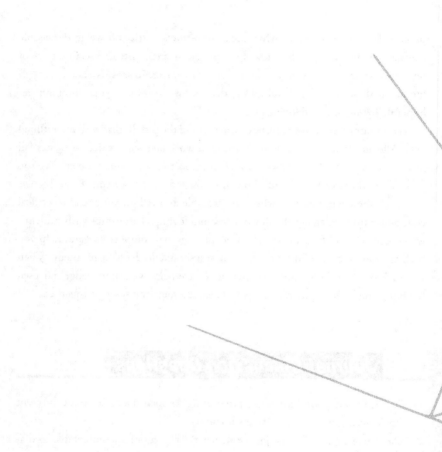

REFLEXIVITY: CHAFING AT OUR LIMITS IN THE COMMUNICATION CLASSROOM

> *IF REFLEXIVITY IS WHAT ENABLES US TO PERCEIVE HOW WE ARE BOTH PRODUCTS AND PRODUCERS OF COMMUNICATION, OF STRATEGIES AND TACTICS, IF REFLEXIVITY IS WHAT ENABLES US TO PERCEIVE THE STROKE AGAINST THE WAVE, THEN IT WILL BE, BY NECESSITY, A PERPETUALLY UNSETTLING PROCESS.*
>
> FASSETT AND WARREN (2007, P. 86)

I TRUDGE THROUGH THE SNOW, MENTALLY CURSING HOW COLD IT IS AS I WALK TO THE COMMUNICATION STUDIES BUILDING FROM MY CAR. My shoes make a slight crunching sound as the ice under the white powder cracks and crumbles beneath my feet. By the time I reach the door, my face is red and wind-chapped from the cold north wind howling through the campus. As I walk in and the wave of pleasantly warm air hits my face, I wonder what "genius" thought living in this hellish cold-scape was a good idea—especially since Carbondale was founded long before the sweet comfort of central heating.

I proceed from the entrance up the stairs, waving and offering a short, but hearty, "Hello, friend!" to other graduate students as I go. I make my way to the department's office to check my mailbox. Looking inside, I see a thick manila envelope labeled "Instructor Evaluations" from the (cue dramatic sound—BUM! BUM! BUM!) Center for Teaching Excellence. A chill runs through me. *"What if they are bad? What if I don't get to teach again next semester?"* I think to myself.

I hurry out of the office to find an empty hallway where I can look at the evaluations in private. I find a spot without traffic, but ready access to a restroom in case I need a good cry if my evaluations are as negative as I fear they will be. My eyes dart in either direction—nope, no one is around. I open up the envelope and, mustering all my courage, look over the document inside.

The evaluation is on heavy paper, much larger than the regular 8.5 × 11 pages I typically use. The printing is from an old dot matrix printer, reminding me of the printers I used when I was in elementary school. I scan the pages, looking at the numbers that range from 0 to 5: "Organized—4.5"; "Available for Outside Consultation—4.7"; "Gave Helpful Examples—4.5." I relax as I go through the list, there's no rating less than a 4.0, so I don't think my job is in jeopardy.

I shake my head in amazement when I see some of my lower scores, "Stayed Consistent with the Syllabus—4.0." "Why is that even an item?" I think to myself. "And, is that a good score or bad score?" Students in the class had seemed interested in the topic of sexual violence on college campuses, so I spent an extra week holding class discussions, showing video clips, team teaching, and providing resources to students who needed services from or wanted to volunteer at the local women's center. Was I not supposed to do that? Was adhering to the syllabus more important? Or, would an administrator commend me for breaking from the plan to meet students where their interests, and needs, lay?

As I get to the end of the evaluation, I read the final item: "Overall Effectiveness as an Instructor—4.7." "Great," I think to myself. "I'm a 4.7 teacher. Now what the heck does that even mean?"

****

As you consider what kind of instructor you want to be, we encourage to you think about the steps you will take to realize your pedagogical goals. Will your materials center marginalized voices about communication issues? How will you walk the fine line between pushing students out of their comfort zone and explicitly calling them out? How will you know that your course promoted social justice learning goals? These are questions that every instructor, new and continuing, is faced with. Each of these questions, and many more, require us to think not just about what we do, but why we do it, and what logic, values, or experiences we use to assess some questions, rather than others, as worthy of conversation.

Even though instructor evaluations are supposed to help instructors identify their weaknesses and attempt to improve, we find they often focus on matters of effectiveness rather than on social justice. We wish to be clear, being an effective instructor is important—being prepared, organized, and enthusiastic as an instructor can have a strong, positive influence on students' learning (Dannels, 2014). However, like Kyle R. in the story, we are often left scratching our heads about the questions asked, and the answers given, in many of the university-created instructor evaluations. We ask: To what end is an instructor effective? For example, we do not think that effectively teaching good communication skills only from a predominantly White cultural perspective (which often masquerades as "objective" dos and don'ts) is an ideal you should strive for in your teaching. In our opinion, the classroom dynamics that are most important are those that help realize, as both a process and a goal, social justice through meaningful and engaged learning. Our emphasis on that ethic puts us on the path to recognizing the importance of reflexivity.

Reflexivity, as articulated by Freire (2000), refers to the ongoing process of understanding one's situatedness always in relation to, and in dialogue with, others. Reflexivity is more than just confessing to subjectivity or reflecting back on the positions that make up your intersecting identities (e.g., I perform White, heterosexual, learning disordered, first-generation college student, poverty-class female). It is "a thinking about thinking ... that inherently takes our contemplations and meanings further out, beyond our own mirrored gaze" (Madison, 2006, p. 322). We do not believe that reflexivity is something that someone can be (e.g., I am a reflexive teacher); rather, it is an ethic that people strive to practice in their lives. Reflexivity within the teacher–student relationship can help foster the caravan, Conquergood's (2002) metaphor for "radical democracy and difference where fellow travelers are deeply and meaningfully interacting with one another" (Madison, 2011, p. 129). Reflexivity challenges instructors to be better to and for others (and themselves), and celebrate their vulnerability as an ethic of humility and love. In this chapter, we utilize the concept of reflexivity to outline ways that you can practice *allying* with non-dominant/marginalized group members in and beyond the classroom. After explaining our understanding of allying, we argue that trust, vulnerability, and faith (in the Freirean sense) are three ways to begin explicitly engaging in reflexive relationships in the classroom.

reflexivity
the ongoing process of understanding one's situatedness always in relation to, and in dialogue with, others

allying
the process of working with, and deferring to, marginalized communities to realize social justice

ALLY(ING)

In our examination of literature, we have found that many authors write about ally(ing) as either identity (e.g., I am an ally) or as action (e.g., I'm allying with marginalized people). Authors who argue for an ally identity often posit developmental models for identifying, interrogating, and challenging their privilege (e.g., Hardiman, Jackson, & Griffin, 2002). These frameworks document the transition from having little or no sensitivity, knowledge, or experience with a marginalized group to exhibiting a deep investment in the struggles of that group. By positing ally as an identity, the authors are able to make the claim that one's ally identity intersects with other social identities, shaping and constraining one's ability to perceive and act against oppression. For example, a cisgender Latino can be a strong advocate for his ethnic community while still perpetuating anti-trans violence if he does not develop his identity as an ally to trans folk. These authors' work encourages instructors to work to unlearn oppressive understandings of groups they do not identify with or belong to, while working in solidarity with them on issues that are important to their community.

Although we certainly see the merit in understanding ally as an identity, we encourage you to work toward an ethic of allying (as a verb) rather than being an ally (as a noun). Much like our admonition that reflexivity should not be thought of as a static goal, we do not believe that understanding oneself "as an ally" is the most productive way of engaging in social-justice education—without working to perform allying, you can't create an ongoing, socially just relationship. We find that people who think of themselves "as an ally" often use that identity to shield themselves from the criticisms from the people they purport to serve. When called out for doing or saying things are oppressive, these individuals often become very defensive and refuse to take responsibility for their actions. They deny their complicity in oppression by uttering statements such as

1. Ashley was so angry when she disagreed with my comment about Black Lives Matter. Why doesn't she like me?
2. Loretta walked away from me when I said *he* instead of *hir*. I don't know why he has to be so sensitive all the time!
3. Tony said that I have class privilege, but I work at the homeless shelter every weekend. What else can I do to get rid of my privilege?

When privileged people make statements such as these, it serves to elide their responsibility to engage reflexively with communities they work with in their advocacy. As Rodriguez (2015) argues, those who believe they inhabit an ally identity often damage the communities they are supposed to be allied with by being more concerned with building or maintaining their credibility as a "good ally" than with working in *solidarity* with oppressed people. Although certainly you will find joy and meaning as you teach for social justice, you should also recognize that allying with people in a marginalized community will be an unsettling and sometimes painful process that disrupts your taken-for-granted assumptions about power, privilege, and oppression (Fassett & Warren, 2007).

> **solidarity**
> the ethic of standing with marginalized communities, even (especially) when doing so may result in social, economic, or physical punishment

Allying is not about getting gold stars, certificates, or "likes" on Facebook™ for the work you do as a social justice educator. Quite rightly, Rodriguez (2015) labels these activities "ally theatre," arguing that a person with privilege concerned with the topic of advocacy must learn how to do their work without needing to be applauded as the "good privileged person" (see also Thompson, 2003). McKenzie (2014) offers some guidance on how to start thinking reflexively about your allying work:

1. Do not assume one act of solidarity makes you an ally forever.
2. Do not make everything about your feelings.
3. Do not try to date people different from you to show your openness.
4. Do not erase other's identities (e.g., I never noticed you were Asian!).
5. Try to include non-dominant people in your classes, activism, and performances. No, really, try. Try harder.
6. Do not just rely on interpersonal forms of activism (e.g., calling out a student's racist remarks). Work toward dismantling institutionalized oppression.
7. Do not just take in the work of non-dominant folk (e.g., go to the local queer of color film festival). Contribute to making sure those events happen.
8. Do not quote famous non-dominant people (e.g., Audre Lorde or Dr. Martin Luther King Jr.) to assert that a marginalized person's activism is wrong or misguided.

In other words, allying with marginalized people means that *their* needs, experiences, and knowledges come first. If your first reaction to having your advocacy challenged by members of a marginalized community is to deny or explain away their concerns, then you are most likely using their pain as a stepping stool for your own advancement within society (e.g., "Oh, look at how much she cares about homelessness! Isn't she such a great person?"). Remember, framing identities as a communicative performance (see Chapter 2) should be a consistent reminder that social-justice education is something you *do*, not something that you *are*.

Our understanding of allying is based on the belief that doing ally work is a continuous commitment. As such, there is not a quality or quantity of social justice activities that one engages in to be an ally or earn an ally identity; rather, each moment of advocacy is its own, unique opportunity to realize a social-justice ethic within that particular time, place, and cultural context. Within each moment of allying in the classroom, we ask you to continuously practice three ethics as a social justice educator: vulnerability, trust, and faith.

VULNERABILITY

When Kyle R. teaches the introductory communication course, he assigns students an identity essay. Students are supposed to write about two of their positionalities (e.g., class, race, sexuality, or gender) and recount the ways they talk, perform, or do their culture. One semester, Kyle used an essay from a previous year, where the student wrote about his White, male privilege and the ways he acts that reinforce his privilege, as an example of a good paper. Kyle thought the essay, in addition to being well-written and thoughtful, demonstrated a person grappling with the issues of privilege and oppression in their life (something he wanted his students to do in their essays). However, a few African American female students approached him after class and told him that they were having trouble writing their essays. When he asked why they were having difficulty and pointed them to the example essay, they asserted that the essay did not make sense to them. One asked, "How am I supposed to write about being White and male? How is this supposed to be an example for me?" Kyle realized

whiteness

a system of belief that positions White identity (and its cultural values, attitudes, and characteristics) as neutral, natural, or normal (e.g., I'm not White, I'm human), even as White experiences, values, or beliefs are privileged within society through conversations with the students that by giving only one example that was rooted in White experiences (even if it was a critical interrogation of White experiences) he had re-centered *whiteness* by excluding other cultural examples.

To be vulnerable is to recognize that you will fail as a social justice educator at some point (or, more realistically, at many points) during your lifetime. Whether you cut off students' exploration of a topic in order to cover ground, use a textbook that is not culturally relevant or aware, or give an off-the-cuff example that uses non-inclusive language, you will find that you are not, and cannot be, a "perfect" social justice advocate. And, rather than despair at the thought that you will never "get it right" (especially because the mindset of right and wrong does not fit evaluations of this type of work), we believe you should find strength in embracing your vulnerability as a place where you can learn—learn from your students in ways that model a humble spirit.

The ethic of vulnerability is best encapsulated in Maya Angelou's statement, "I did then what I knew how to do. Now that I know better, I do better." Although Kyle added more examples for the assignment that included a wider range of positionalities, he is not off the hook for his complicity in racism or sexism (Johnson, 2006). Doing "better" does not mean perfecting social-justice practice. He has made and will continue to make errors as he strives to teach for social justice. As you strive to be a good social justice educator, and make your own failures (and feel those painful struggles) along the way, remember that it is in those failures that you learn how to grow and do better for yourself and others in the classroom.

Vulnerability can also be a powerful method of leading students towards cultivating a reflexive ethic. Throughout this book, you have read stories from our classrooms that reflect both successes and failures. Too often, we feel that allying is about sharing our successes and working towards helping others find success of their own. On the other hand, we recognize that sharing stories and reflections about our failures can assist others in creating spaces to learn from, and not simply be embarrassed by (and, admittedly, ashamed of), their own failures. Coming into a *critical consciousness* is a lifelong process, filled with failures that feel like successes and successes that feel like failures. Finding a way to communicate both sides of the process is critical to help students recognize how their own behaviors can be both productive and harmful in their own journeys of awareness.

> **critical consciousness**
> the habit or disposition of interrogating power, of always asking, "Who benefits and who is left out by the decisions being made?"

It is natural to feel shame, anger, frustration, fear, and even despair as you engage in ally work in the classroom; however, we ask that you 1) fully recognize and engage those feelings; 2) learn to do better rather than make excuses or repress them; and 3) recognize your responsibility as a social justice educator. An important component of embracing your vulnerability is to talk about your struggles with your students, peers, and mentors. We do not mean you should continuously burden others through selfish confession as a way to alleviate your own guilt or shame, and thereby elide your responsibility to grow and learn. Rather, we believe you should recognize that our partialness and fallibility as social justice advocates calls us to rely upon our communities. Our communities need to include others who, in relation to you, are different, thereby risking moments of critical contact and cultural confrontation, but also expanding your circle of knowledge and empathy (DeTurk, 2011). It is our belief that the need for vulnerability demands that we, as social-justice educators, refuse the possibility, or even the aspiration, of being a perfect social justice advocate, because such a person would no longer need a community. A central part of being vulnerable is listening, truly and authentically listening, to the accounts and responses of marginalized peoples. Doing so is an important step in cultivating the next ethic: trust.

TRUST

During our years of teaching, we have heard colleagues tell new graduate student-teachers and instructors to "take command of the classroom" and "force students to respect you." They often caution young teachers that failing to do so invites students to "walk all over you" and runs the risk of surrendering professional authority. We recognize that the role of a teacher is a position of authority and that respect is an important component of good teaching relationships and practices. Furthermore, teachers from marginalized identities may face threats to their credibility based on perceptions about their identity and may need to more intentionally incorporate communicative strategies that establish respect (e.g., Patton, 1999; Russ, Simonds, & Hunt, 2002). In short, there is nothing inherently wrong about wanting to cultivate an ethic of respect for yourself with students in the classroom. However, we caution you against viewing control or intimidation as necessary ingredients for learning. We believe such an ethic devalues students as it frames them as little more than unruly animals in need of the civilizing force of the teachers' expertise and direction. Instead, we believe you should cultivate an ethic of trust with students that establishes respect but does not secure it through reinforcing hierarchy and teacher-centered knowledge distribution.

Trust refers to the notion that students have a wealth of knowledge at their disposal that instructors should meaningfully incorporate into the class in ways that promote growth and change for everyone in the classroom. This ethic means that instructors should be willing to allow students to pursue their own choices, and learn from other students as they explore those areas, within the class to nurture their growth as self-directed, confident, and motivated change agents. In our experience, too many teachers try to incorporate student experiences simply as a means to gain student investment in the course material. Although certainly this may be an outcome of this practice, we do not believe that this embodies an ethic of trust. Trust, to us, does not refer to ways of getting students to comply with instructors' wishes through concessions or bribes. Rather, it signifies a need for instructors to let go of control and authority and allow students to direct their learning in ways that you may not have foreseen.

Although we encourage you to trust students, we often struggle to embody this ethic. For example, Kyle R. teaches a course on social justice communication activism and mass incarceration, in which he asks students to volunteer with local prison reform/abolition groups. This year, a student asked to create a student organization for prison education rather than volunteer at an existing organization. At first, Kyle encouraged the student to adhere to the syllabus and find a prison education advocacy group. He felt the student, a senior in his last semester, might want to create his own group as a way to minimize his work and slack off until graduation. However, the student was adamant and continued to ask Kyle for this assignment; he eventually relented and let the student pursue his ambition. Over the next few weeks, the student contacted other students and membership for this group expanded to over two dozen students in a few short weeks. The group wrote letters to administrators and legislators, and even developed a schedule for hosting a mini-conference on prison reform and education. In short, Kyle's need for control and his lack of trust almost ruined the opportunity for these students to pursue their own learning and achieve success on their own terms.

An ethic of trust does not mean that you should be gullible—students are people and people lie, misrepresent, and misremember things. Trusting students means that your first instinct should be to recognize and affirm them as they navigate the classroom or university environment. This ethic is particularly necessary when interacting with students from marginalized groups. We have heard colleagues state that some students "just aren't college material" and, whether they recognize it or not, those utterances are all-too-often directed at students of color, or those from poverty. These instructors feel that they are "defending high standards" by not recognizing the knowledges and experiences that marginalized students have; instead, they maintain that the culture of higher education is correct, normal, or neutral, and students should strive to conform to the institution's standards.

As Yosso (2005) argues, this type of thinking is predicated upon a *deficit narrative*, or the idea that marginalized students are not good enough to meet the standards of normal (read: White, middle/upper class) society (see also Solorzano & Yosso, 2001). She goes on to assert that marginalized students, rather than being deficit, hold a great deal of cultural knowledge that is not typically privileged in society, such as linguistic capital (e.g., being multi-lingual), resistant capital (i.e., persevering despite oppression), and familial capital (i.e., finding social support in family relationships). We encourage you to explore, with students, the ways that they wish to work toward social justice and to trust them in their efforts to be sincere, authentic, and motivated change agents. Doing so will lead you to places you could not have anticipated—places where you and students can learn and grow together.

deficit narrative

the idea that institutions of education are primarily fair, equal, and just places, and that the disparities between groups (e.g., White and Black students) are due to the lack of hard work or inferior culture of the marginalized groups

FAITH

The final ethic we hope you cultivate as you ally with students is a strong sense of faith—faith that the world can change and change for the better. Having faith in students, and yourself, as capable of changing and growing toward a more socially just world requires a *utopic vision*. As Leonardo (2009) states,

> The idea of utopia is integral to human educational progress because it guides thought and action toward a condition that is better than

current reality, which is always a projection. ... *Critical education* is no less than the search for a language of utopia. (p. 24)

Sometimes it might feel like having faith is an exhausting, even naïve, ethic. In a world where people of color, people from poverty, people who identify as LGBTQ, and/or female are increasingly being attacked on all sides—from access to clean water in Flint, Michigan, to the shutting down of women's health clinics across the United States—it is hard to maintain faith in people's ability or willingness to strive for a better world. And, the sad fact is that we often have trouble maintaining our faith. Learning about mass incarceration, the state-sanctioned murder of people with disabilities, or the ways that people profit from the United States' illegal and immoral wars against other countries makes it hard for us to imagine how our classrooms can have any effect at all on the problems that face us as a nation and a species.

> **utopic vision**
> an aspiration for the most socially just outcome in any and all situations

Sometimes, students test our faith. When Kyle R. was months into teaching his class on communication activism and mass incarceration in the United States, one student referred to restorative justice, a peace-building justice rather than the punitive system that the United States currently relies on, as a "bunch of unicorns farting rainbows." In those moments, sometimes counting to ten and taking deep breaths does not assuage the feelings of hurt, loss, and frustration. The student— White, male, and middle class—did not even recognize the pain that the U.S. justice system has wrought on marginalized communities, believing that each victim of police brutality—people like Eric Garner and Sandra Bland—deserved their fate. In moments like those, when students refuse to even recognize the dignity of people and the cruelty of the system and their words, we find it hard to muster the energy to talk about or even imagine that the world could be a more humane place.

It is easy to become bogged down, worn out, and disillusioned in your quest to realize a social justice ethic within and beyond the classroom. But we, along with other social justice scholars, encourage you to dream and work toward a utopic vision. As Darder (2002) asks, "How poor is a revolution that doesn't dream?" (p. 93). We are reminded by Solnit (2006) that often evidence for social justice activism is in what did not happen, rather than what did, as a result of utopic dreaming: a male didn't resort to physical or verbal abuse with his partner (resisting patriarchy), a

White person didn't accept a prestigious position and created a space for an equally (perhaps, even more) deserving person of color (resisting whiteness), or a cisgender person stopped using transphobic language (resisting cisgenderism). Each of these instances, and more, are sometimes invisible, making it easy to believe that social justice education has no influence on peoples' hearts or minds. We become seduced into thinking that change only occurs in large demonstrations and give up on seeing victories, both large and small, as a part of an ongoing project to realize hope in the face of seemingly impossible odds.

A critical, rather than an unthinking, faith asks us to recognize and embrace the hope that things can and should be better now—that we should not wait another second to realize a world where things are more socially just. At the same time, a critical faith cautions us to avoid the burn out, reminding us that the road is long and self-care is an important part of ensuring that we engage in sustained, healthy advocacy (Horton & Freire, 1990). As you continue on your road as a social justice educator, strive to find, for yourself and with others, a sense of balance between a relentless desire to see the world become a more humane place and not leading yourself, or others, into harm through a narrow-minded or nonreflexive focus. Doing so will help you keep your critical edge sharp, while creating sustainable, nurturing, and loving relationships and communities with others.

CONCLUSION

We started this book by talking about how John mentored us to be better critical teachers, scholars, and people. As we read and reread his work—published manuscripts, old emails, and scribbled notes on the class papers and books he left behind—we feel a deep sense of grief that we will never again get the chance to drink a pinot noir while listening to a local band with him on a hot southern Illinois evening. Because of John, and the work that he devoted himself to, we believe that our insights are stronger and our hearts bigger. We hope you will be the kind of mentor that John was to us for the peers and students you have the privilege to interact with during your higher education experience.

In one of his last published works, John wrote about the power of love, reflexivity, and justice in the communication classroom. He stated:

> A [philosophy of love] cannot end at the classroom wall—we are all people of the world and as such, we must be willing to be transformed, speaking back to the world from this newly humbled and humanized location. It is a vision for being that is worth the effort to actualize. (Warren, 2011, p. 33)

We, too, believe that a vision of the world as a more loving, humane, and just place is worth the effort to actualize. And, even though there is so much—too much—wrong with our world, we hope that you will join us in the struggle of leaving it a better place: one classroom, one day, and one student at a time.

Journal/Discussion Questions

1. How does a socially just world look, sound, taste, smell, and feel?
2. How can you create an education (through your classes or career) that works to realize such a world?
3. What assumptions did you make about students in your class?
4. How did the community environment of the classroom influence ways in which you could have connected to the student(s) and the student(s)?
5. How do you see your work in the classroom connecting to your advocacy for social justice outside of the classroom?

SOCIAL JUSTICE CLASSROOM ACTIVITIES FOR THE COMMUNICATION CLASSROOM

IN THIS CHAPTER, WE SEEK TO ANSWER JOHN AND DEANNA'S CALL TO ARTICULATE WAYS OF BUILDING BRIDGES BETWEEN THEORY AND PRACTICE IN THE COMMUNICATION CLASSROOM (FASSETT & WARREN, 2007; WARREN & FASSETT, 2011, 2014). Before moving on to the activities, Kathryn (the primary editor of the activities section) wanted to use this space to show our process of calling for, reviewing and evaluating, and collaboratively co-vising the submissions. Our objective for this transparency is to practice a commitment to demystifying the culture of power that surrounds academic writing and publication, and to be honest about our struggles as authors and collaborators.

To begin the process of soliciting submissions, Kyle R. emailed our activities call to the Communication, Research, and Theory Network (CRTNET), which is the National Communication Association's (NCA) email listserv. He also created and distributed flyers during division business meetings at the communication conferences we annually attend (the National Communication Association in fall and the Central States Communication Association in spring, both great places to meet other scholars, teachers, and activists).

Together, Kathryn and Kyle R. had planned one month to gather submissions and two to three weeks to review and confirm the final evaluations of the activities. In reality, gathering submissions took one and half months, and reviewing and evaluation took twice as long as planned. If anyone reading this has ever been part of a process of reviewing scholarship, you will understand some of the frustrations that come with staying organized and responsive with those who are submitting their work.

In the end, we received over 50 activity submissions and accepted 16 activities, pending revision work from the authors. Wonderfully, the authors were receptive to feedback and many spoke with us as they revised their work—leading us to characterize our relationship as co-vising rather than simply revising—to ensure that their vision, and ours, were met in each activity. For our take away experience with the reviewing and revising process of publication, we offer this knowledge: If you take the time to commit to a pedagogical process of dialogic collaboration and an ethic of care for the complexity of critical communication pedagogy and social justice pedagogy, the results will (more often than not) be better than what you thought was possible.

CRITICAL COMMUNICATION PEDAGOGY AND SOCIAL JUSTICE OBJECTIVES FOR THE COMMUNICATION CLASSROOM

We chose communication activities based on their use of social justice frameworks, variety of content and theme, reflexivity, and adaptability for new graduate-student teachers and instructors of critical communication pedagogy. Specifically, we chose activities that met the following goals:

- The authors attempted to construct the activities with explicit connections to Fassett and Warren's (2007) work with critical communication pedagogy, social justice, difference, oppression, and/or power.
- To help connect these activities to one another, and to the scholarship of communication pedagogy as a family of knowledge, we encouraged authors to use the recently developed National Communication Association (2015) Learning Outcomes in Communication (LOCs). We recommended a critical connection to the objectives under outcomes 5, 7, 8, and 9.

- We asked authors to be as concrete as possible in explaining the ways that students (and instructors) engaged in reflexive thinking as they worked together to expand their cultural perceptions and assumptions through the activity.
- We asked authors to view culture as a site of contestation (i.e., whose culture is valued), rather than something that everyone simply has (i.e., we are all different).
- As it is important to bridge the theory and praxis of critical communication pedagogy, we challenged authors to tie their activity to a formative or summative project or assignment that would be appropriate for an introductory communication course.
- To support the relationship between critical communication pedagogy and social justice, we worked toward incorporating various ways that students might challenge the systemic dimensions of oppression, rather than only filling an immediate or short-term need within their communities (e.g., a single or unengaged act of charity or community service).

ACTIVITY 1

EXPLORING SOCIAL JUSTICE THROUGH PERSONAL NARRATIVE

JACQUELYN ARCY

RATIONALE

The social justice narrative speech assignment asks students to deliver a four-to-six minute speech about a social justice issue that is relevant to their lives. In narrative form, students tell a true story about either: 1) their own experience with social privilege and oppression, or 2) an experience or event that altered their perspective on a social justice issue. Student speeches span topics such as immigration, race, class, gender, sexuality, nationality, dis/ability, bullying, healthcare, food deserts, and climate change, to name just a few examples.

Social justice narrative speech assignments are often used in the Introductory Communication Course because the creation process may help students learn how to construct a story, communicate key ideas, and organize a speech. By focusing this assignment on social justice, students also learn how to communicate with an ethical intention and appreciate cultural difference. This assignment deploys the critical communication methodology of autoethnography that, according to Fassett and Warren (2007), "demonstrates the power of examining personal experiences in order to understand culture" and "explore our own roles in making the social structures that bind us" (p. 47).

Using a critical pedagogical perspective, this assignment asks students to situate their own experiences in relation to larger social, cultural, and economic structures, to better understand structures of social issues such as racism, sexism, classism, and homophobia. When students name and narrate their experiences with privilege and oppression, they learn to practice a radical reflexivity or "the interrogation of the self" (Fassett & Warren, 2007, p. 50). Also, as students listen to their classmates' experiences with racism, sexism, and other forms of oppression, they learn about difference and begin to question taken-for-granted assumptions about social structures and stereotypes. In this way, the assignment fulfills the central feature of social justice pedagogy that "challenges, confronts, and disrupts misconceptions, untruths, and stereotypes that lead to structural inequality and discrimination based on race, social class, gender, and other social and human differences" (Nieto & Bode, 2008, p. 11).

COURSE:

Introduction to Public Speaking

OBJECTIVE(S):

In accordance with the National Communication Association's *Learning Outcomes in Communication Project* (NCA, 2015), this activity serves the following objectives:

- Students learn to "apply ethical communication principles and practices" (LOC 7) and to "influence public discourse" (LOC 9) by using storytelling techniques to raise awareness and effect social change.
- Students "demonstrate the ability to accomplish communicative goals" (LOC 6) by performing effective verbal and nonverbal public speaking skills.

ACTIVITY

Preparation for this assignment is made up of two 50- or 75-minute class periods that introduce and model a social justice narrative. Then, students deliver a four-to-six minute speech in class. For a class of 25 students, this activity will span two 75-minute class periods or three 50-minute class periods.

DAY ONE

Introduce students to the social justice narrative speech assignment by reviewing the assignment sheet and rubric.[1] It is helpful for the instructor to model this type of speech by delivering his or her own social justice narrative based on a personal experience. Next, familiarize students with the basics of narrative speaking using the different types of stories elaborated by Marshall Ganz (2007) in his essay "What is Public Narrative?"—"story of self," "story of us," and "story of now"—and emphasize how narrative connects personal stories to shared values that motivate others to act.

Next, engage the class in a discussion of Ganz's essay, using the following discussion questions:

- How do public social justice narratives inspire advocacy action?
- What emotions are most powerful to motivate change?
- What storytelling devices are effective for mobilizing emotions? Why?
- How does your public narrative seek to change your audiences' perspective?

DAY TWO

Screen Leslie Morgan Steiner's (2012) TED Talk titled "Why Domestic Violence Victims Don't Leave." Explain to students that this is an effective example of a social justice narrative speech and lead them in a dialogue to identify the key elements of social justice narratives, including plot, character, setting, and the moral framework.

DAYS THREE TO FIVE

Days three to five (depending on how many students you have) should be used for the performance of students' social justice narrative speeches.

---

1   The assignment sheet and rubric are available at available at goo.gl/4BMeZO.

DEBRIEFING

After the speeches are finished, debrief with students by discussing the following:

- Which speeches were you most affected by and why?
- Which storytelling devices were most effective in evoking change?
- What social justice issues did you find most compelling?
- In what ways are you motivated to take critical action in relation to any of these causes?

REFLEXIVE APPRAISAL

By delivering and listening to stories about systemic and cultural injustices, students are led to new ways of understanding and navigating the world. The critical value of this assignment lies in its transformative potential, encouraging students to embrace social justice as active participants, defined by Sonia Nieto (2010) as "a philosophy, an approach, and actions that embody treating all people with fairness, respect, dignity, and generosity" (p. 46). A limitation for this assignment is that it is not prefaced with a unit on social justice concepts and readings. I encourage instructors to integrate concepts such as social privilege, systemic oppression, and social justice into the Introductory Communication Course throughout the semester to help prepare students for the challenge of this assignment. Another potential challenge is that students can struggle to come up with a personal story related to a social justice issue involving their privileges and oppressions. In these instances, I have advised students to tell the story of a family member or friend (with permission), as it is sometimes easier, when attempting to reflect on these issues, to think about a relatively close person, rather than one's own experiences. However, I do encourage instructors to challenge students to use their own experiences, which may cause them to see their own histories differently.

REFERENCES

Fassett, D. L., & Warren, J. T. (2007). *Critical communication pedagogy*. Thousand Oaks, CA: Sage Publications.

Ganz, M. (2007). *What is public narrative?* Retrieved from http://comm-org.wisc.edu/syllabi/ganz/WhatisPublicNarrative5.19.08.htm.

NCA. (2015). *Drawing learning outcomes in communication into meaningful practice*. The National Communication Association's Learning Outcomes in Communication Project. Retrieved from https://www.natcom.org/sites/default/files/publications/LOC_2_Drawing_Learning_Outcomes_in_Communication.pdf

Nieto, S. (2010). *Language, culture, and teaching: Critical perspectives* (2nd ed.). New York, NY: Routledge.

Nieto, S., & Bode, P. (2008). *Affirming diversity: The sociopolitical context of multicultural education* (5th ed.). Boston, MA: Allyn & Bacon.

Steiner, L. M. (2012, November). Leslie Morgan Steiner: Why domestic violence victims don't leave [Video file]. Retrieved from https://www.ted.com/talks/leslie_morgan_steiner_why_domestic_violence_victims_don_t_leave?language=en.

VIRTUALLY "SPENT": ENGAGING EMPATHY THROUGH A CLASS PRIVILEGE ONLINE GAMING SIMULATION

ERIKA BEHRMANN

RATIONALE

About 15% of the U.S. population falls below the poverty line (Bishaw, 2013). In a classroom setting, students with poverty or working class backgrounds may not have access to the basic school materials (books, computers, transportation, etc.) nor fundamental needs (food and shelter) to do well in school. Moreover, conventional portrayals of the middle-class college student fail to capture the lived experiences of those who do not fit this mold. Selman-Killingbeck (2006) speaks to this erasure in her work and how she used various "survival strategies" to get through college as a working-class woman, such as modeling others' behaviors, overcompensation, and engaging in behaviors of resistance. Yet these issues are rarely discussed in a classroom setting. Even in courses that focus on theories of race and gender, socioeconomic status is often forgotten (Roberson & Zlotnick, 2010).

In the communication classroom, the traditional, middle-class student often struggles to understand how socioeconomic privilege shapes communication. For many students, this might be the first time someone has challenged them to reflect upon and talk about their socioeconomic status and the spectrum of power related to where they are positioned. For some, it can be incredibly difficult to talk about, whether they struggle to see their privilege or struggle to negotiate their lived oppressions. Due to these reasons, I have used the educational video game *Spent* as a resource to galvanize dialogue with my students about class issues. *Spent* can be used as an alternative to other privilege-based activities, such as the well-known privilege walk activity, which encourages students to disclose personal information to their peers. If used in conjunction with other materials, it is an effective way for students to discuss class privilege/oppression and systematic inequity without forcing students to "out themselves" to others in the class.

It is important to note that *Spent* gives a mere snapshot of what living in poverty can be like. This game should only serve as a stepping stone into the complex discussion of class issues and socioeconomic status ideologies in the United States. This activity asks students to play the online game *Spent*, during class or at home, and then respond to a variety of discussion questions that focus on issues of privilege/oppression and how the experiences in the game relate to their own lived experiences with their class background. This activity takes one class period (50–75 minutes) with outside class prep.

COURSES:

Introduction to Communication; Communication and Culture

OBJECTIVE(S):

After this activity, students will be able to:

- define socioeconomic status and identify examples of class privilege,
- demonstrate an intellectual and ethical awareness of classism and its effects on everyday lived experiences, and
- be able to achieve the following learning outcomes in communication (NCA, 2015):
  o identify ethical perspectives and propose solutions for (un)ethical communication (LOC #7),
  o demonstrate the ability to be culturally self-aware (LOC #8), and
  o advocate a course of action to address local, national, and/or global issues from a communication perspective (LOC #9).

ACTIVITY

INTRODUCTION OF ACTIVITY

- Prior to class, students should read Chapter 3: Public Advocacy from Warren and Fassett's (2015) *Communication: A Critical/Cultural Introduction.*
- Students are asked to complete the following prompt prior to the activity: Describe a time that you were aware of your socioeconomic status.

REVIEW OF CONCEPTS (10 MINUTES)

- Ask students to describe what socioeconomic status means.
- In class or online (depending on course format), students can share their answers to the previous prompt. **Note:** Because this requires a certain amount of trust between students, I typically allow people to volunteer their answers. Also, it is incredibly valuable to hold yourself, as an instructor, accountable for your own class positionality. This vulnerability can build trust with your students and make the space more comfortable for sharing this information.

PLAY *SPENT* (30 MINUTES)

- Have students go to the website www.playspent.org.
- The game will challenge the student to make it through a month without going broke. Given only $1,000, students are asked to make difficult spending decisions. For example, one of the first prompts asks students to choose between putting the family dog to sleep or pay for veterinary bills (which would be the equivalent of an entire month's rent). Another example is: Do you let your child go to a birthday party with a gift or do you save money?
- Students will need to play until they "lose."

DISCUSS FINDINGS (20 MINUTES)

- The following question prompts are adapted from Gaw's (1979) Processing Questions: An Aid to Completing the Learning Cycle.

Experiencing:
- What did you observe?
- How did this game make you feel?

Sharing:
- How many examples of class privilege were you able to identify?
- Are there any examples of class privilege that you might not have known about prior to playing this game?

Interpreting:
- What do you think the developer felt during the process of creating this game?
- What is the purpose of this game?

Generalizing:
- What does this game suggest to you about class privilege and communication?
- Does this video game remind you of any experiences that you might like to share?

Applying:
- How does this relate to Warren and Fassett's understanding of privilege and public advocacy?
- What might you do to help challenge class privilege through public advocacy?

ADVOCACY (AS MUCH TIME AS YOU CHOOSE)

The final step to this activity is rooted in public advocacy (the theme of Warren and Fassett's chapter) and the chapter's notion of praxis (putting theory to practice). This final part of the activity asks students to write an advocacy paper and apply what they have learned in class to their own lives. After the activity, give students the following prompt:

In Chapter 3, Warren and Fassett argue that "reflexivity involves situating ourselves as part of the phenomenon or problem we are working to describe" (p. 46). Using the ideas outlined by Warren and Fassett (pp. 245–248), I want you to select one of the tactics listed below and discuss how you might use that tactic to create positive change in terms of socioeconomic class and privilege. Give specific examples from your everyday life.

Tactics: advocacy through 1) reflexivity, 2) dialogue, 3) critical literacy, 4) listening, 5) speaking up, and 6) alliance building

DEBRIEFING

Due to the fact that the game is structured so players "lose" (as a critique of the current capitalist systems we live in), often students will lose within five minutes, so I typically have students play until they get through the entire month. Although winning serves no purpose to the game, you want students get as far as possible. This is primarily because students who lose early miss out on becoming familiar with the later prompts in the game and the difficult decisions they have to make.

REFLEXIVE APPRAISAL

This activity offers critical value by unveiling socioeconomic class privilege. Students who play this game typically begin to recognize how socioeconomic class assumptions shape their perceptions of themselves and others. Furthermore, this activity steps toward a discussion about the pitfalls of meritocracy and capitalism. Despite this, it is important to note that the game does not offer an intersectional perspective of identity. As such, instructors who use this game are encouraged to complicate the game with more information about the complexities of other identity markers on class privilege/oppression.

REFERENCES

Bishaw, A. (2013). *Examining the effect of off-campus college students on poverty rates.* Retrieved from the U.S. Census website: https://www.census.gov/library/working-papers/2013/acs/2013_Bishaw_01.html

Gaw, B. A. (1979). Processing questions: An aid to completing the learning cycle. In J. Jones & W. J. Pfeiffer (Eds.), *The 1979 annual handbook for group facilitators* (pp. 147–153). San Diego, CA: Pfeiffer & Jones.

NCA. (2015). *Drawing learning outcomes in communication into meaningful practice.* The National Communication Association's Learning Outcomes in Communication Project. Retrieved from https://www.natcom.org/sites/default/files/publications/LOC_2_Drawing_Learning_Outcomes_in_Communication.pdf

Roberson, K., & Zlotnick, S. (2010). Putting class back in the women's studies curriculum. *Feminist Teacher, 20*(2), 95–110. doi:10.1353/ftr.2010.0007

Selman-Killingbeck, D. (2006). Can a working-class girl have roots and wings? White trash in the ivory tower. In S. L. Muzzatti & C. Vincent (Eds.), *Reflections from the wrong side of the tracks* (pp. 61–68). Oxford, UK: Rowman & Littlefield Publishers, Inc.

Warren, J. T., & Fassett, D. L. (2015). *Communication: A critical/cultural introduction* (2nd ed.). Thousand Oaks, CA: Sage Publications.

ACTIVITY 3

ENGAGING SOCIAL JUSTICE EMPATHY THROUGH INTERPERSONAL COMMUNICATION

KEVIN JONES AND BETHANY WIDDICOMBE

RATIONALE

Fassett and Warren (2010) identify 10 key commitments for critical pedagogy, and this exercise fulfills several of those commitments. The authors argue "that good communicators should know how identity is constructed in communication, how critical communication educators embrace social structural critique as it places concrete, mundane communication practices in meaningful context, and reflexivity is an essential condition for critical communication pedagogy" (p. 377). This activity demonstrates to students how identities can be constructed by the unethical language and destructive discourses people use in every day communication. This activity shows how mundane communication like a simple expression (e.g., "that is so retarded") not only creates inequality but also forms social injustice.

Segal (2011) identifies the need for greater social empathy to combat social justice topics. The challenge to connect empathy to social justice often lies in the misperception that social justice is only a global issue involving human rights issues around the world (Kemp-Graham, 2015). Recent scholarship (Fassett & Warren, 2007) has called for a reframing of social justice to understand it as a local, daily personal topic including experiences such as sexist or racist jokes, homophobic slurs, mental illness shaming, bullying/cyber bullying, along with so many others. Laughing at a rape joke is seldom seen as similar to a person being imprisoned in another country for their religious beliefs, yet both are forms of social injustice.

COURSE(S):

Introduction to Communication; Interpersonal Communication

OBJECTIVE(S) (NCA, 2015):

- Students will understand that social justice is not just a global issue, but social justice issues are also local and on a personal, daily level.
- Students will demonstrate the ability to be culturally self-aware and adaptive to diverse cultural contexts through communication.
- Students will learn to recognize the influence of different messages and demonstrate mindful responses with an ethic of care.
- Students will analyze and present proposals for solutions to unethical communication.

ACTIVITY

Overall, this lesson should take between 45 and 50 minutes for activity and debriefing. Begin the activity by asking the class to define social justice. The goal for this step is to try to come to some sort of consensus on what the phrase means. Students can write the definitions in their notes before the instructor asks some of the class members to share their answers. While the students openly share, the instructor or a designated person can write the key words or phrases on the board. Generally, the key terms that emerge have to do with global issues such as racism, poverty, oppression of women and people of color, silencing of marginalized voices, and many others. The goal is to recognize that social justice revolves around bringing empowerment to voices that are otherwise unable to be heard (Rinehart, Barbour, & Pope, 2013).

After a brief discussion defining social justice, place the class in small groups of four to five students. Ask each student to 1) identify a time when they hesitated or were afraid to speak up when someone said or did something that hurt their feelings, made fun of them, or made them feel part of an outside group; or 2) identify a time when they observed or saw someone being hurt by something being said or done to them and did not respond. Have each student identify what was said or done, how they felt when it happened, why they did not respond on behalf of themselves or the person they saw being hurt, and whether or not they continue to think about the incident.

After sharing in groups, ask the students to write down what could have been said or done to address what happened. Have each person share with their group what could have been done to address the situation. This type of sharing can create some very vulnerable moments, so it is best to keep the sharing in small groups and not share answers with the class. The goal of this portion of the activity is to encourage students to identify what it feels/felt like to be in a situation where they were uncomfortable or unsafe when not speaking up or voicing the issue.

After each group has finished sharing their stories, the instructor should give a brief discussion on the definition and meaning of empathy. Not everyone engages empathy in the same way, but there is a need to see the situation through someone else's perspective. Segal (2011) defines social empathy as "the ability to understand people by perceiving or experiencing their life situations and as a result gain insight into structural inequalities and disparities. Increased understanding of social and economic inequalities can lead to actions that effect positive change, social and economic justice, and general well-being. It is built upon individual empathy" (pp. 266–267). This definition can be used as a starting point for this discussion.

Ask each group to brainstorm as many ways as they can think of in which people are minimized, belittled, or diminished on a daily basis. Start by giving a prompt, such as, "What about when people call something gay or retarded?" Let the groups brainstorm for a few minutes, then go around and ask each group to share what they came up with. Write some of the topics on the board. When each group has shared, ask the entire class: "In each of these examples, whenever 'that's so retarded' or '_____' (fill in the blank with examples on the board) is said: How can you be an ally for the oppressed group? How can we stand up for marginalized people?" Reconnect the earlier example of the empathy that each student wished would have happened when they saw or experienced an injustice. That same ethic of empathy is needed on both the global level and local level for social justice.

DEBRIEFING

If time allows, you can ask each group to brainstorm ways that they can speak out when they see, hear, or experience a local social injustice. For example, when they hear someone say, "I have a great Black or woman joke for you," they can start by responding with a simple "no, thank you." However, that is not enough. The person making the unjust statement can be told how language shapes reality and how language creates social injustice. Other topics may be more difficult to discuss gracefully, but that is part of the goal for this activity. Solutions to these difficult issues require extended dialogue. Have each group share some of their responses with the class.

REFLEXIVE APPRAISALS

This activity can show students how identities of social justice are constructed by the words we communicate and that even the simplest of expressions has the potential to create harm on a much larger scale than we realize. Social justice is so often seen as a large, global issue, but this activity can reframe social justice within the everyday use of language. Trying to change mindsets creates a potential barrier for this activity. Trying to identify the harm in everyday, seemingly innocuous statements can create an uncomfortable or defensive climate for many students. The instructor should be prepared to create a supportive, confirming climate and mandate the use of confirming language by all participants in the activity.

A large limitation of this activity is time constraint. The activity can easily fill a 50-minute class period if each group engages and talks. Debriefing can be lengthy, depending on how many groups you have. Smaller groups (3–4 people) tend to foster more discussion (safer environment), yet can create seven to eight groups in a class of 25 students. Debriefing takes more time if you want to go around the room and have each group share with the class. Larger groups (5–6 people) create fewer groups, but the larger group size can inhibit discussion. Each instructor should know the culture of their classroom and know what approach would be best for their class.

REFERENCES

Fassett, D. L., & Warren, J. T. (2007). *Critical communication pedagogy*. Thousand Oaks, CA: Sage Publications.

Fassett, D. L., & Warren, J. T. (2010). *The SAGE handbook of communication and instruction*. Thousand Oaks, CA: Sage Publications.

Kemp-Graham, K. Y. (2015). Missed opportunities: Preparing aspiring school leaders for bold social justice school leadership needed for 21st century schools. *International Journal of Educational Leadership Preparation, 10*(1), 99–129.

NCA. (2015). *Drawing learning outcomes in communication into meaningful practice.* The National Communication Association's Learning Outcomes in Communication Project. Retrieved from https://www.natcom.org/sites/default/files/publications/LOC_2_Drawing_Learning_Outcomes_in_Communication.pdf

Rinehart, R., Barbour, K. N., & Pope, C. C. (2013). *Ethnographic worldviews transformations and social justice.* Dordrecht, the Netherlands: Springer.

Segal, E. (2011). Social empathy: A model built on empathy, contextual understanding, and social responsibility that promotes social justice. *Journal of Social Service Research, 37*(3), 266–277. doi: 10.1080/01488376.2011.564040.

ACTIVITY 4

THE COHORT EFFECT

NICK CHIVERS

RATIONALE

The rationale for this activity is grounded primarily in Fassett and Warren's (2007) *Critical Communication Pedagogy*. Identities, self-image, cultural values, and our perspectives of our social worlds are created, maintained, reinforced, and challenged through our communication practices. These communication practices form complex systems of power, privilege, and oppression, and can range from highly formalized, stylized, and politicized communication events (e.g., political campaign speeches, written law) all the way down to common, mundane, everyday utterances (e.g., interpersonal conversation or social media interaction). From this critical communication pedagogy perspective and a social justice perspective, we see that social, cultural systems and our identities within them are created through communication, and these systems are founded on a fluid system of power and oppression.

Therefore, it is through analysis and deconstruction of our individual and everyday communicative choices that we can begin to dismantle these systems of oppression and work to recreate new, more equitable and just social realities. It is critical communication pedagogy and a social justice orientation that creates the praxis of communication theory in our everyday lives. There is no better place to address this praxis than in an introductory communication or fundamentals of communication course. By critically analyzing our everyday linguistic practices, this perspective can create competent and ethical speakers who are equipped to engage in social justice discourse in their public addresses as well as their everyday lives.

COURSES:

Introduction to Communication; Public Speaking; Intercultural Communication

OBJECTIVES:

- Students will locate how, in their daily lives, their discursive practices are implicated in the process of co-constructing social worlds; that their language is laden with their cultural values; and that the use of language perpetuates those values.
- Students will analyze messages, especially those in their everyday interactions, and use this analysis to understand and employ mechanisms of ethical communication practices.
- Students will deconstruct the ways in which language creates difference, and then use their language to embrace difference.

ACTIVITY

First, this activity should be used to exemplify and amplify any discussions of the power of verbal communication and language practices as they relate to cultural values, biases, and the shaping of social worlds. Second, this activity can get quite energetic, borderline chaotic—it tends to be helpful to warn the students that this will happen, and although it is designed to be very energetic and engaging, there will be moments where you will need to maintain some order to hear students' voices.

1. Divide the class into groups of three to four students. This is generally a good opportunity to allow members of the class to interact with folks they may not have worked with before.
2. Ask each group to brainstorm as many words as they can that either a) did not exist or b) meant something different 10 to 15 years ago (one generation older). It helps to set a timer (5–10 minutes) to add a sense of urgency to their brainstorming.

3. After the time has expired, ask each group to "rank" their words on whatever criteria they deem most appropriate (most commonly used, most impactful, etc.). Have each group create a "top 10" list. **Note:** Set another short timer for this part. Don't let the students overthink it; the precise ranking is not crucial to the overall activity.

4. Once every group has their top 10 list, create a master list for the class on the board by asking each group, one by one, to submit their top.5 words. Ask all the other groups to continue editing their list quietly as a group, specifically crossing words off their list that have already been submitted, but also perhaps adding words that are triggered by the rest of the class's submissions.

5. After you have received 5 words from every group, ask them for any final submissions that must be on the board. All totaled, you should have approximately 50 words, submitted by the students, that either did not exist or meant something different for the previous generation.

DEBRIEFING

Up to this point, this activity has likely felt like a party in the classroom—high energy, very raucous, and quite a bit of laughter. It is important to refocus the class on the fact that this was all for a purpose—remind them of the principals of social construction and linguistic relativism. To that end, lead the class in the following discussion questions.

1. WHAT PATTERNS DO YOU SEE IN THE WORDS THAT ARE ON THE BOARD?

    Recently, the words submitted by the students have fallen into three categories: web speak (acronyms such as lol, dgaf, til, hbd; also shortened words, such as obvi, totes, fam, sup), terms created or re-appropriated for the tech industry or for use with technology (e.g., follow, like, hashtag, tweet, and post), and language indicating excess and indulgence, partying, or dance (e.g., finna turnt, fire, twerk, ham, and molly).

2. WHAT DO THESE PATTERNS REPRESENT IN YOUR SOCIAL
    CONSCIOUSNESS OR CULTURAL VALUES? WHAT ASSUMPTIONS ARE
    BEING MADE OR BEING PERPETUATED?

Some trends in discussion tend to revolve around sexist language (if some of
the terms have male heterosexual privilege connotations, like "smash it" or
"bang it"), or classist language (the use of tech and web speak [e.g., follow
me on Vine] assumes universal access to social networking technology).
Also, there tends to be a lack of politically current terms (ISIS, LGBTQ+,
Tea Party, Democratic Socialist, etc.), indicating an infantilization or at least a
distancing of youth from political activism.

3. HOW DO THESE LINGUISTIC PATTERNS NORMALIZE CERTAIN CULTURAL
    VALUES AND MARGINALIZE OTHERS?

Again, the language operates to normalize partying, enhancing sensory experience, drug use, consumption, and, by extension, capitalism, hegemony, and
neoliberalism. If a diverse classroom comes up with 50 words that speak to
the experience of White, able-bodied, heterosexual, middle-class males, the
language itself serves to normalize this experience and marginalize all others.
Furthermore, the perpetuation of these language patterns creates ingroups
and outgroups: Those that have the language skills, the economic access, and
the leisure time to fully engage in pop culture through the use of social media
are "in," while others (others within the classroom community) are "out."

4. LANGUAGE, CULTURAL APPROPRIATION, AND POWER:

a. Do you know any words or phrases from other languages that do not
    translate directly to English? How do these phrases highlight differences in
    cultural values?

All the words contributed are going to be in the language of the class
(English, if we are in the United States). Phrases such as L'esprit de l'escalier,
Schadenfreude, and other similar phrases highlight the reflective nature
of language and cultural values. If a language doesn't have a word for these

experiences, do the people of that cultural group experience them? Or experience them to the same extent?

b. Do you know any words or phrases that English speakers have appropriated from other languages? What is the implication of this practice for issues of power and privilege?

Appropriating words from other languages, severing them from their intended cultural context, and using them to serve our own cultural context (e.g., "Drinko De Mayo") solidifies the power of English in larger cultural context—English speakers engage in these practices because they can without consequence. This further entrenches English-speaking cultures in positions of power.

c. What words or phrases do we use that have been separated from violent histories? How is the use of these words perpetuating systems of power and privilege?

Many words in our common vernacular have their roots in various systems of power (e.g., "ghetto" and "nigger" with White supremacy, "bitch" with patriarchy, "fag" with heteronormativity, and "tranny" with cisnormativity), and our appropriation of these words into common discourse without fully understanding their implications of violent histories works to maintain these systems of power, and create violent cultural conditions for the identities they marginalize.

5. HOW CAN WE ADJUST OUR LINGUISTIC PATTERNS TO CREATE A MORE JUST AND EQUITABLE SOCIAL WORLD?

This is where I bring up historical examples, such as "sexual harassment," "marriage equality," and "blacklivesmatter." We also discuss something as mundane as androcentricity (default to the masculine; e.g., saying "you guys" or "mankind"). Also, we discuss violent and dangerous linguistic trends, such as

- illegal = dangerous and unlawful = Mexican,
- terrorist = violent and murderous = Muslim,
- thug = criminal and violent gang member = Black man,
- bitch = female dog = woman; and so forth.

Discuss the power of these words in creating social realities for certain marginalized populations, and potential alternatives to realize a better social world.

6.   PLAN OF ACTION REFLECTION PAPER:

As a follow up to this activity, assign a short reflection paper asking each student to apply these concepts to the students' own lives. Use any combination of the following prompts:

a.   Engage in a close reading of the previous 24 hours of your social network, preferably something textual or video based, be it Facebook, Twitter, Yik-Yak, Vine, or any others, and analyze the language of one particular post. Consider the social position of the author of the text, and discuss how the language of that social media post works to construct social realities for themselves and others.

b.   Read or watch one production of local daily news and analyze the language used in a particular news article or news segment. Discuss how the language used to describe this news event simultaneously creates a framing for understanding and engaging with our social worlds.

c.   What are some potential linguistic pitfalls you may encounter in an upcoming speech? Why would they appear in your speech? Why should you avoid them? What could you potentially replace them with and why would these be a better option?

REFLEXIVE APPRAISAL

This activity has proven to be quite fun for students. It is high energy and very engaging, and works to bring abstract concepts home to the lived experience of the audience. It resembles social research—applying communication theory to a particular data set—and as the students have provided all the data used for analysis, they recognize how their behaviors and their lives are implicated in the findings. Also, it gives the students agency to make meaningful changes in their own worlds. It can be a slightly uncomfortable and difficult class dynamic for an instructor to navigate—there are times when I feel like I am losing control of the classroom, and there are times in which this activity makes me vulnerable, since some of these words being presented I simply do not know. Even though the instructor may be vulnerable and not have complete control, during the activity it is important that the class maintains focus on how the mundane and daily communicative practices relate to larger discursive formations. It's a bit of tricky dance.

However, as the normalized position of power within the classroom, it is crucial to critical communication pedagogy that the instructor participates in this discomfort. This activity functions to destabilize that power, for a time marginalizing the instructor, and can in turn highlight the ways in which language affects cultural formations and systemic power structures. Also, in considering marginalization, I try to encourage non-traditional students and international students to contribute to discussions based on their experiences, and also contribute their perspectives as a somewhat marginalized identity in the context of the normalization of the cohort's language. However, it is crucial to be careful not to tokenize these students, making them the sole voice of the populations they are representing.

ACTIVITY 5

ENCOURAGING DIFFERENCE THROUGH EVALUATING JOB LISTINGS AND MISSION STATEMENTS

ALISON M. LIETZENMAYER

RATIONALE

This assignment is designed for students to identify how change can occur in organizations, and how organizational policies influence the trajectory of social justice. Further, this assignment helps direct students in how to use critical skills to evaluate organizational policies with the intent to embrace difference and create a more inclusive work team. Students learn about their spheres of influence and are able to recognize the need for change in organizational policies and recruitment endeavors. This assignment provides a process for approaching change within systems they might participate in during their careers. Students have the chance to see the how their own spheres of influence are a form of power, and how they can be mindful of the companies they work in (and look for opportunities to assist in the redirection of organizational policies to promote and embrace an inclusive work environment across a range of social identities; Allen, 2011a; Fassett & Warren, 2007). Given in the last quarter of the semester, this assignment asks students to synthesize and apply theory from across the course and demonstrate an understanding of the intersection of organizational communication and social identity theory as it relates to social justice.

COURSE(S):

Interpersonal Communication in Organizational Contexts; Professional Communication

OBJECTIVE(S):

- The student will be able to identify difference-negating language, as well as make inclusive critiques for incorporating difference-affirming language into organizational job listings or mission statements.
- The student will illustrate their analysis in the form of an audiovisual presentation, which will demonstrate the inclusion of communication theory, terminology, and course content.
- Furthermore, in line with the National Communication Association's (2015) learning outcomes in communication (LOCs; NCA, 2015), this assignment requires students to practice skills outlined in LOC 5: Critically Analyze Messages, and LOC 8: Utilize Communication to Embrace Difference.

ACTIVITY

Instructors should review the following topics ahead of giving this assignment: ideal worker, difference in the workplace, and social identity within Chapters 1, 2, and 9 of Allen's (2011b) text.

DIRECTIONS

1. Find *five job listings* designed for a manager role (upper, mid-level, etc., are all acceptable). Then, find the corresponding *mission statement* for the organizations. (These might be called a mission statement, vision statement, or culture statement—be flexible with the title in order to find what students need. Examples will be provided.)[1]

---

1   The following examples are provided to students:
- http://www.seasonalservices.com/about-us/our-vision,-values-and-culture-statements/
- http://www.edelman.com/careers-and-culture/culture/company-culture/
- http://www.thyssenkrupp.com/en/nachhaltigkeit/unternehmenskultur.html
- http://www.ogilvy.com/About/Our-History/Corporate-Culture.aspx
- http://www.boeing.com/boeing/aboutus/culture/index.page

2. After you have found various organizational job listings and corresponding mission statements, you should read, or reread, Chapters 1, 2, and 9 of *Difference Matters* (Allen, 2011b).

3. Critically evaluate the job listings and mission statements as they relate to: organizational culture and communication, interpersonal communication, and organizational communication.

   a. This assignment follows the belief that "even as communication reinforces dominant meanings of difference, communication facilitates social change" (Allen, 2011b, p. 185). Deconstruct messages (job listings and mission statements) to identify how communication is being utilized to *facilitate social change* or (if it doesn't) give suggestions for an organization to alter their language in order to recruit workers to a difference-affirming workplace.

4. Analyze the job listings and mission statements using course materials and Allen's (2011b) *Difference Matters* reading to answer the questions below for each organization. Then, design a presentation that includes audio recordings to share your analysis.

   a. While I encourage students to be creative in how they approach this presentation, it should be formal (verbally citing sources to support their claims), well-organized (easy for a viewer to follow—incorporating verbal transitions, a clear introduction, and a conclusion within the audio recording/s), and founded in communication topics and theory (i.e., showing a clear connection to the course materials and Allen's (2011b) *Difference Matters*).

5. Answer the following questions for all five job listings and mission statements chosen:

    Organizational Culture Analysis:
    -   Does the job listing acknowledge difference? If yes, how so? Is difference affirmed or discounted in some way?
    -   Does the job listing identify communication practices, standards, or expectations within the organization? If yes, how so?
    -   What does the mission statement tell a potential worker about the organizational culture or work climate?

    Evaluation:
    -   What are the highlights or potentially the bestselling points of the job listing? The mission statement? (What is attractive about the company to a potential worker?)
    -   Suggested revisions or considerations: If the job listing or mission statement does not address communication, use the course materials and Allen (2011b) readings to make at least two suggestions for how the job listing *and* mission statement could more to directly affirm difference in order to attract workers.

    Job Listings/Organization Statements:
    -   This could be where students get creative: five job listings and mission statements from the same industry (clothing brands, tech industry, etc.), or five job listings and mission statements that are from different industries but use similar language or expectations to attract potential workers. Students should identify these theme(s) as they complete their analyses.

DEBRIEFING

After the project is submitted, students are required to write a summary discussion board post identifying their findings and sharing observations about the project or language utilized in mission messages. Reflective writing such as the summary work of this assignment, as noted by Alvarez, Bauer, and Eger (2015), "encourages reflection about various ways of thinking/feeling/behaving in their current organization" (p. 305). Although the authors refer to blogging, this assignment reinforces their assertion that "reflexive pedagogical practice facilitates deeper understanding of difference in organizations and encourages an activist voice that empowers students to see themselves as potential agents of change and not bystanders within a larger system of exclusion" (p. 306). After the assignment is completed, students have the opportunity to continue the dialogue of why this work is necessary and relevant to an organization wanting to cultivate an inclusive working environment. This dialogue is hosted in a separate ongoing class discussion area where the instructor can monitor the dialogue as needed, engage ideas, or provide additional resources.

REFLEXIVE APPRAISAL

The project has been a success in the past three semesters it was assigned. Noted limitations or challenges were the need to direct students on how to find or identify appropriate organizational statements after choosing job listings, and guiding critical engagement with such complex communication issues. Instructors must provide appropriate information and resources to students to indicate how difference-affirming language and communication can be used to direct change within an organization. This type of work is key for the communication classroom because of the types of careers communication students might accept and their potential role in drafting or directing such language in organizational settings. Students appreciate the reflection component of the work and gaining experience in organizational writing, as well as engaging in critical communication with their peers.

REFERENCES

Allen, B. J. (2011a). Critical communication pedagogy as a framework for teaching difference and organizing. In D. K. Mumby (Ed.), *Reframing difference in organizational communication studies: Research, pedagogy, practice* (pp. 103–125). Thousand Oaks, CA: Sage Publications.

Allen, B. J. (2011b). *Difference matters: Communicating social identity* (2nd ed). Long Grove, IL: Waveland Press.

Alvarez, W., Bauer, J. C., & Eger, E. K. (2015). (Making a) difference in the organizational communication undergraduate course. *Management Communication Quarterly*, 29(2), 302–308. doi: 10.1177/0893318915571352

Fassett, D. L., & Warren, J. T. (2007). *Critical communication pedagogy*. Thousand Oaks, CA: Sage Publications.

NCA. (2015). *Drawing learning outcomes in communication into meaningful practice*. The National Communication Association's Learning Outcomes in Communication Project. Retrieved from https://www.natcom.org/sites/default/files/publications/LOC_2_Drawing_Learning_Outcomes_in_Communication.pdf

ACTIVITY 6

EXPLORING HOW COMMUNICATION IS CENTRAL TO SOCIAL JUSTICE ACTIVISM

DAVID L. PALMER

RATIONALE

Education research suggests that when students are cast as active citizens, their learning outcomes improve and they develop durable commitments to civic participation (e.g., Levinson, 2012). Yet, education rarely teaches students about social justice causes or how to participate in those causes. One alternative is to have students explore social injustices and how communication is central to struggling against those injustices. As students explore the role communication plays in social activism, they also explore a variety of social justice causes, and incentives to get involved in those causes (Frey & Palmer, 2014).

COURSE(S):

Introduction to Communication; Organizational Communication; Communication and Social Justice Activism

OBJECTIVE(S) (NCA, 2015):

- Identify the challenges facing communities and the role of communication in resolving those challenges.
- Utilize communication to respond to issues at the local, national, and/or global level.
- Advocate a course of action to address local, national and/or global issues from a communication perspective.

ACTIVITY

This lesson can be implemented as a unit plan or as part of a larger semester-length project that examines social justice activism. First, students examine a variety of communication-based activities that social justice organizations recommend as effective forms of civic activism. Second, students construct and present a persuasive speech that is designed to elicit direct public participation in a specific social justice cause.

REQUIRED MATERIALS:

In-class Internet access, preferably screen projected

PRELIMINARY STEPS

1. Instructors should review sources that outline strategies for getting involved in social causes. Online examples include (a) DoSomething.org, (b) Gene Sharp's 198 Methods of Nonviolent Action, and (c) the American Association of Colleges and Universities.
2. Instructors should review social justice organization websites that outline clear steps for getting involved in social causes. Examples include (a) Oxfam .org, (b) Equalitynow.org, and (c) Sierraclub.org.
3. To prepare for this project, students are required to complete a brief, typed report that outlines the following information. Students should have two copies of this report: one to submit to the instructor and one to use as a discussion resource.
    a. Employ a keyword search (e.g., social problems, social issues, and social injustices) to compile a list of five social injustices that you find worth exploring.
    b. From that list, choose one injustice about which you are passionate. Research and discuss what the problem is, some of its causes, and why you are passionate about it.

c.   Locate and list three organizations that are tied to that social injustice. Online examples include (a) Oxfam.org, (b) Equalitynow.org, and (c) Sierraclub.org.

d.   Identify and discuss the strategies that those organizations suggest that people can use to get directly involved in their social cause. For example, most justice organization websites have a tab titled Take Action, Get Involved, or Volunteer.

Focus on the communication-based actions that they outline; for example, write letters to a local paper and to your senator, create a discussion forum at your school, and volunteer for local organizations.

IN-CLASS ACTIVITIES

To examine social justice causes and participation strategies, and incentives tied to those causes, consider posing problem-solving questions to students, as opposed to using a lecture format (see, e.g., Freire, 2000). As students and instructors explore social injustices and how to get involved in social causes, they develop ideas, strategies, and problem-solving skills that they can employ in beyond-the-classroom social activism projects. The below activities are designed to guide students as they prepare to design and deliver their culminating persuasive speech.

1.   **Examining social injustices.** Generate class discussion about the reports that students have compiled. Discussion prompts should include the following:
   • Share your list of five social injustices with the rest of the class.
   • Which social injustice did you choose, and why are you passionate about it?
   • What is the nature of the problem, and who does it primarily impact?
   • What are some of the causes of the problem?

2.   **Identifying social activism micro-goals.** Given that no individual or justice organization can eliminate a social injustice, such as poverty, one sensible tactic is to identify achievable micro-goals that support larger solution initiatives tied to the injustice. Discussion about these micro-goals should be located at the regional and national levels. Common activism micro-goals could be
   • raise public awareness,
   • change minds locally,
   • raise and donate money,

- change or support relevant local and national policies,
- create or help develop social justice advocacy communities, and
- advocate for and vote for regional and national politicians who are sympathetic to the cause.

Questions to prompt discussion may include the following:

- What is a social activist?
- Why is it prudent for activists to focus on small, achievable goals as opposed to huge, overwhelming goals?
- How might these micro-goals help support broader efforts to solve social problems?
- How might these micro-goals support the social cause that you have chosen?

3. **Examining justice organizations and the communication-based participation strategies that they recommend.** Discuss the social justice organizations and "How to Get Involved" tactics that students have located. To fill in the discussion, share with students the activism tactics that you located in your pre-project research. Examples include: social media and media activism, art activism, community building, theater activism, and coordinating and/or participating in a peaceful protest. Discussion topics may include the following:

- What social justice organizations did you find that are actively working to change the social injustice in which you are interested? Tell us about them.
- What *communication-based* "How to Get Involved" tactics did you discover as you examined the organization websites tied your chosen social justice cause?
- Which of these participation tactics appeal to you as a critical agent of change, and why?
- How is communication central to these tactics? That is, how are these tactics grounded in our understanding of communication?
- What impact do you believe that these tactics or strategies can have on the larger project of social change in your chosen issue?

4. **Examining incentives for public participation.** To help students envision and employ persuasive incentives that can be used to elicit public involvement in social justice activities, help them develop compelling arguments for direct participation, such as

- public involvement as a necessary feature of social justice solutions,
- activism as fulfillment of a moral duty and social responsibility,
- activism as a form of networking and community building, and
- activism as the belief for social change in action.

Discussion topics may include the following:

- Why is simply donating money to social causes not enough to solve social problems?
- Is widespread public participation in these social causes necessary to create real and lasting changes? Explain.
- Why might people in general not directly participate (or hesitate to directly participate) in social justice causes?
- What arguments might be used to persuade people to directly participate in social cause activity? What persuasive tactics would be effective to get people involved?

5. **Persuasive speech assignment.** Students are required to develop and present a persuasive speech to the class (and/or in a public venue) that is designed to elicit direct public participation in the social cause that they have chosen. I recommend that, if possible, students first present their speech to the class as a preparatory phase for presentation in a public venue of their choosing. The public presentation is a powerful learning experience that invites students to see themselves as real-world justice advocates (Palmer, 2004). Public presentations can easily be videotaped on a cell phone and reviewed by the instructor and, if desired, by the class.

    One recommended persuasive speech format is Monroe's Motivated Sequence (Ehninger, Monroe, & Gronbeck, 1978). Evaluation of the persuasive speech—beyond standard speech evaluation criteria—should assess how effectively students outline the following information:

    a. <u>Attention</u>: an enticing introduction to the problem, a central thesis, and a speech preview

    b. <u>Need</u>: an outline of the nature of the problem, the need for systemic change and public participation beyond charity to help solve this problem, and compelling reasons that people should get involved

c. Satisfaction: a summary of the communication-based strategies that justice organizations tied to the problem recommend for public participation

d. Visualization: an outline of the impact that these participation strategies can and do have on the larger efforts to eliminate the social problem

e. Action: a summary of clear steps that audience members can employ to develop and implement one or several of these communication-based participation strategies

DEBRIEFING

One effective conclusion to this assignment is to dedicate in-class time to student discussion about their speech research, design, and implementation experiences. I find that students want to discuss the social injustice and activism-related content that they have discovered as they prepared for and delivered their speeches. The time immediately following student speeches is ripe for encouraging them to take the next steps needed to get involved in their chosen social cause. I encourage students to contact the justice organizations that they have researched and to design and implement in their community one or several of the communication-based strategies that they outlined in their persuasive speech.

REFLEXIVE APPRAISAL

I find this lesson plan to be an inspiring invitation for students to explore social causes, to connect to organizations that are passionately dedicated to solving social problems, and to explore the communication-based tactics that people can use (and compelling reasons to use them) to support larger efforts to eliminate social injustice. Because so much of their education experience is detached from the lived world of social problems and activist activity, students are sometimes hesitant to view themselves as real-world advocates for social change. To offset this misperception, I consistently challenge students to view themselves as social-change activists whose efforts are directly impacting the world of social justice change. I remind students that the civil rights movement, for example, was successful not simply because Martin Luther King Jr. was a powerful leader and speaker, but more so because of the committed daily hard work of millions of unheralded civil rights activists. As a result, this social activism project has proven to be a transformative experience for many of my students.

REFERENCES

Ehninger, D., Monroe, A. H., & Gronbeck, B. E. (1978). *Principles and types of speech communication*. Glenview, IL: Scott, Foresman.

Freire, P. (2000). *Pedagogy of the oppressed*. New York, NY: Continuum.

Frey, L. R., & Palmer, D. L. (Eds.). (2014). *Teaching communication activism: Communication education for social justice*. New York, NY: Hampton Press.

Levinson, M. (2012). *No citizen left behind*. Cambridge, MA: Harvard University Press.

NCA. (2015). *Drawing learning outcomes in communication into meaningful practice*. The National Communication Association's Learning Outcomes in Communication Project. Retrieved from https://www.natcom.org/sites/default/files/publications/LOC_2_Drawing_Learning_Outcomes_in_Communication.pdf

Palmer, D. (2004). Employing civic participation in college teaching designs. *College Teaching*, 52(4), 122–127.

ACTIVITY 7

GETTING CRITICAL COMMUNICATION
PEDAGOGY "ACCEPTED"

USING A POPULAR CULTURE PORTRAYAL OF THE
EDUCATION SYSTEM TO ENCOURAGE RADICAL
CRITIQUE OF THE BANKING SYSTEM

JULIE L. G. WALKER AND KATIE MARIE BRUNNER

RATIONALE

Students spend years learning how to navigate the U.S. education system. From elementary school through high school, students are socialized into becoming passive receptacles for schools to deposit information (Warren & Fassett, 2011). Freire (1970) discusses the concept of banking in the system of education and calls for more emancipatory pedagogies as ways of freeing students from the oppressive structure of schooling. He calls for an interactive model of education where teacher and student work together, liberating the classroom and potentially creating opportunities for co-constructed knowledge and meaningful realities. McLaren (2003) illustrates how "the dominant culture is able to exercise domination over subordinate classes or groups" not by using force, but rather "through consensual social practices, social forms, and social structures produced in specific sites such as the church, the state, the school, the mass media, the political system, and the family" (p. 76). Shor (1996) argues that higher education, particularly for lower-class students, represents an environment of unequal power relations, developed to keep them in subordinate positions in society. Aronowitz (2003) argued that the purpose of higher education has solely become just the way to prepare us to enter the labor force; to "accept work as a mode of life; one lives to work, rather than the reverse" (p. 113). Higher education as a social structure promotes, rather than subverts, this dominant ideology. Ultimately, the current education system not only disempowers students within the classroom, but reinforces them to subserviently exist within capitalist power structures that control the opportunities within their daily lives.

Indoctrination into a grade-focused, standardized-centered banking discourse creates a sense of security in a flawed system that emphasizes testing and deemphasizes learning. Despite frustration with and critique of these systems, when presented with an alternative (namely, critical communication pedagogy) students may seek the system they know best. Smith (1994) noted, "Some students, especially those who are unfamiliar with anything outside of the traditional classroom, feel uncomfortable with the student-centered teaching style" (p. 16). The lesson presented here connects student frustrations with the opportunity for emancipatory pedagogy, where they can reacquire power over their learning.

COURSE:

Introduction to Communication; Basic Communication Course

OBJECTIVES (NCA, 2015):

- Apply and critique communication theories, perspectives, principles, and concepts.
- Differentiate between various approaches to the study of communication.
- Articulate one's own cultural positionalities and work to deconstruct the effects these positionalities have on one's communication and worldview.
- Identify the challenges facing different communities of culture and analyze the role of communication toward the resolution of those challenges.

ACTIVITY

GETTING TO KNOW YOU

On the first day of class, we give students a questionnaire based on Shor's (1996) work. The survey is designed to get to know each student as a person, rich with responsibilities outside of class, prior knowledge of communication, and an awareness of ways they can make the world better (see Appendix A). As teachers, we write our own personal answers to the questions while they are answering questions, because Shor acknowledges the power distinction of asking students to complete personal questionnaires without also making ourselves vulnerable and answering the same questions. We then have students form a large circle with the desks and we all share parts of our answers. We give students the choice to share as little as just their name to as much as their full set of answers. In addition to starting to build community, we also ensure all students' voices are provided the space to be heard the first day of class. hooks (1994) stresses the importance of building spaces where all voices are encouraged to speak out, so we try to ensure students are given spaces where they can speak if they choose.

CRITICAL COMMUNICATION PEDAGOGY AND THE FILM *ACCEPTED*

After students begin thinking about what they might be expecting out of the class, about topics that interest them, and start to introduce them to one another, we introduce the concept of critical communication pedagogy (CCP). This can be done in a variety of ways, one of which is through the first chapter of the CCP text or the introductory communication book from Warren and Fassett (2015). Most students in introductory courses have never heard of CCP, and most have spent their entire lives steeped in the banking system of education. While students have critiques of the system, the banking system is where students feel comfortable and safe; it is the system they know. To elicit critiques of the system, we watch scenes from the movie *Accepted* (Bostick & Pink, 2006).

Accepted is a movie featuring a group of high school students who do not get accepted into any colleges they applied for. To avoid telling their parents, they create a fake college through the Internet and by printing official looking documentation, but in the process have also to accept additional applications from hundreds of other students who believe the university to be real. Thus, the runaround to physically stage this fake college ensues. The film ends with the "fake" college getting a probationary education accreditation from the state. We show three scenes from the film: 1) a critique of the standard college classroom (minutes 40:55–44:19), 2) students being asked what they want to learn (minutes 44:20–46:05), and 3) the accreditation hearing at the end of the film (minutes 1:15:08–1:24:54).

The college classroom critique scene shows *Accepted*'s protagonist exploring the "real" college experience by going on a campus tour and sitting in on a few classes at a real college. Students are stressed, they cannot take the courses they wish to take, or they are completely disengaged from class. When the protagonist asks students what they want to learn, students unsurprisingly respond initially by asking what he means. Prior to his question, their educational experiences have been completely outside their control. Students begin exploring their passions, and the protagonist builds learning environments to support their journeys. After the college is accused of not providing true educational experiences purportedly occurring at "real" universities, the protagonist seeks accreditation from the state to substantiate the work the students are doing. The accreditation scene makes a direct comparison between the traditional college model and a college where student interest and desire to learn governs the course content, curriculum development, and pedagogy.

DEBRIEFING AND APPRAISAL

Students enjoy watching *Accepted* because it features actors they know (Jonah Hill, Justin Long, Lewis Black, and Maria Thayer) and the film is funny. Muller (2006) argues that "students are inherently more interested in multimedia—film, television, cell phones, music, and the Internet—than traditional print texts" (p. 32). Humor draws students in, which makes a conversation about educational philosophy and praxis palatable. Students also become uncomfortable with the film, due to their critical reflections on their own experiences with the banking system of education and how the system affects decisions about their futures. After we watch the film segments, we have a conversation about how we learn, what we like about college, and what we would want to see changed. We talk about if they would want to attend a school where they control the classes, and this is the part where they feel most uncomfortable. Students recognize the critiques of college systems, such as being told they cannot take certain classes they are interested in because the classes do not apply to their majors. They recognize classes can be boring when they feel disengaged from coursework. But students also feel incredibly uncomfortable abandoning the systems they know.

Students are able to dialogue with one another about the college experience and what they hoped to learn in (or get out of) our classroom time together. Some students start actively arguing against change. Some students start actively advocating for change. Some students disengage from class because they recognize we will not stop them from disengaging from the conversation. We find students wrestle internally while they negotiate what they have been taught is the "right" way to learn versus the pitfalls of that system; the internal wrestling leads to sometimes palpable discomfort during the discussion. Freire (1970) discussed this phenomenon as the "fear of freedom," where students are so used to the oppressive structure they end up desiring it.

Regardless of where students end up with their feelings about the education system, they are primed to understand why we ask them to work with us to create course policies (such as late work, their expectations for grading timeliness, and attendance policies) and why we ask them about things they want to learn or projects they want to accomplish. For more explicit descriptions of the course policies conversation, Shor (1996) gives examples of negotiating (not giving away) authority in the classroom by "co-developing a syllabus" and "negotiating the curriculum" with his students (p. 18). Typically, a few students end up being active participants seeking more control than others, but other students will voice concerns. We also notice, and Fassett and Warren (2007) agree, that some students are so used to seeking professor approval they try to guess what we want them to say. However, in public speaking class we have had students come up with projects we would never have created, but which complete university-required competencies and are applicable to their lives out of the classroom. Students typically end up mixing traditional structures with the critical pedagogies we attempt to engage. Students seem to appreciate bridging the banking system with strategies that emphasize the creative freedom and power negotiation of an emancipatory education.

While using *Accepted* to help students problematize the banking system of education is an opening to the conversation, there are some limitations to using this approach. One of the major limitations of using *Accepted* to explain CCP is that the film shows a very extreme example of emancipatory education. For students steeped in the ideologies of the banking system (like ours were at the beginning of their undergraduate degrees), including the primary objective to obtain a piece of paper that grants us the opportunities for better jobs after graduation, the film may be uncomfortable or resistance producing. Second, the portrayal of the professions sought by students at the unconventional college were primarily creative positions; no one sought more business-oriented professions such as accounting or administration. Students seeking professional training in certain areas (mainly for money-making jobs in various private sectors) where information expertise is the normative expectation of education success may not see how they relate to arguments the film makes.

For instance, in written reflections students often struggle with and complain about the "boring/anxiety-ridden" lecture-based banking system, but ultimately confess they believe it is the most successful system to get them a job. If students feel emancipatory pedagogies may not be relevant to the standards of potential employers, students may dismiss the ideologies of critical communication pedagogy. Because the film does not address this concern, it should be addressed directly by the instructor. Third, as Fassett and Warren (2007) warned, "specific acts, specific interactions, localized moments are not, in and of themselves, critical communication pedagogy" (p. 115); isolated transgressions are "not always radical nor critical or liberatory" (p. 115). While showing the film may help open a critical conversation, the film is not, by itself, a liberatory solution.

Even for students who struggle with seeing their desired training depicted in the film, the critique of the current college student may encourage more conscious learning aspirations rather than the harmful behaviors (like grade mongering) encouraged by the banking system. For instance, one student noted, "Nobody has ever asked me what I wanted to learn, it's always been more focused around my major and what I can do with it in the future," illustrating the ways students can begin problematizing their own experiences even as they exist within the system. As critical communication pedagogues, we need to remember that we, as hooks (1994) reminds us, must never "surrender the conviction that [we can] teach without reinforcing existing systems of domination" (p. 18). Moreover, watching *Accepted* helped one student have "a better appreciation of how the system, suffocating as it can be, provides a structure upon which we base our society." Having students reflexively analyze their experiences and dialoguing with them about their critiques has the possibility to change the way they learn and live regardless of the content. As one student in a written evaluation said, "I'm really glad we looked at this movie. I am a visual learner and it really helped me connect the concepts that we talked about with my own experiences in college!"

Overall, *Accepted* is a non-threatening way to encourage students to question the banking system of education and their typically unaware, passive role in learning. Their uncertainty regarding change is at least marginally made better by pointing out the invisible, institutional challenges they face throughout their college experience.

APPENDIX A

GETTING TO KNOW YOU ASSIGNMENT

1. What name do you prefer to be called? What pronoun do you prefer I use?
2. Why did you take this course? Why did you specifically choose this section?
3. If you could change one thing for the better about SMSU and your education here, what would it be?
4. If you could change one thing for the better in Marshall, Minnesota, what would it be?
5. Please list one or two major controversial issues currently faced in today's society that you find interesting or provocative.
6. What does "public speaking" mean to you?
7. What questions do you have about public speaking?
8. What do you want from a good teacher? What makes a teacher a good teacher?
9. How many hours do you work each week outside of being a student?
10. How many credits are you taking this term?
11. What types of family obligations do you have this semester?
12. What are your favorite TV shows or movies?

REFERENCES

Aronowitz, S. (2003). Against schooling: Education and social class. In A. Darder, M. P. Baltodano, & R. D. Torres (Eds.), *The critical pedagogy reader* (pp. 106–122). New York, NY: Routledge.

Bostick, M. (Producer), & Pink, S. (Director). (2006). *Accepted* [Motion picture]. United States: Universal.

Fassett, D. L., & Warren, J. T. (2007). *Critical communication pedagogy.* Thousand Oaks, CA: Sage Publications.

Freire, P. (1970). *Pedagogy of the oppressed.* New York, NY: Continuum. (Originally published in 1968.)

hooks, b. (1994). *Teaching to transgress: Education as the practice of freedom.* New York, NY: Routledge.

McLaren, P. (2003). A look at the major concepts. In A. Darder, M. P. Baltodano, & R. D. Torres (Eds.), *The critical pedagogy reader* (pp. 69–96). New York, NY: Routledge.

Muller, V. (2006). Film as film: Using movies to help students visualize literary theory. *English Journal, 95*(3), 32–38.

NCA. (2015). *Drawing learning outcomes in communication into meaningful practice.* The National Communication Association's Learning Outcomes in Communication Project. Retrieved from https://www.natcom.org/sites/default/files/publications/LOC_2_Drawing_Learning_Outcomes_in_Communication.pdf

Shor, I. (1996). *When students have power: Negotiating authority in a critical pedagogy.* Chicago, IL: University of Chicago Press.

Smith, L. (1994). Secret basketball: One problem with the student-centered classroom. *Feminist Teacher, 8*(1), 16–19.

Warren, J. T., & Fassett, D. L. (2015). *Communication: A critical/cultural introduction.* Thousand Oaks, CA: Sage Publications.

ACTIVITY 8

BEYOND THE CLASSROOM WALLS: SHARING INSTITUTIONAL PROBLEMS AND PROPOSED SOLUTIONS AT PUBLIC SYMPOSIA

KRISTOPHER COPELAND AND
AMY ALDRIDGE SANFORD

RATIONALE

Symposia are formal, proscribed discussion formats that allow students the opportunity to explore societal issues and dialogue with an audience (Cragan, Kash, & Wright, 2009; Engleberg & Wynn, 2012). Fassett and Warren (2007), in their book *Critical Communication Pedagogy*, noted that naming a problem or injustice is not enough to create change. They warned that many critical projects disappoint in the end because "they usually offer some final thought that never quite seems to do enough, never seems to respond to the problem they've set out to address" (p. 164). Symposia allow students opportunities to not only name problems, but offer solutions as well. This activity is designed to connect students to critically think about college–community relationships, embrace diversity and difference, and empower students to discuss issues related to social justice.

COURSE(S):

Introduction to Communication; Small Group Communication

OBJECTIVE(S) (NCA, 2015):

This unit activity will help students embrace difference and influence public discourse by:

- identifying and developing an awareness for social justice issues impacting their communities through the practice of group communication and cultural negotiation tactics, and
- utilizing research and public communication skills necessary to identify, analyze, and propose solutions to these problems.

THE ACTIVITY

It takes approximately five weeks to complete this unit. A few recommendations:

- Place the activity at the end of the semester, once the students have gotten to know each other and have explored social justice–related issues (e.g., sexual violence on campus, institutional racism).
- Prior to this unit, it would be helpful to cover content regarding member roles, teamwork, speechmaking, problem solving, and agendas and minutes.
- Allow class time for group meetings.
- Reserve a public space on campus that seats 50 to 100 people and allows for use of technology during presentations.

WEEK 1: UNIT INTRODUCTION

Use Week 1 to explain the purpose and function of group symposia. It is recommended that this assignment is part of a small group communication unit. Discuss how concepts in small group communication (e.g., collaboration, synergy, group roles, etc.) will be important as they work together. Engage the students in a discussion about an assigned reading (e.g., Cragan, Kash, & Wright, 2009; Englebert & Wynn, 2012). Explain that they will need to pick a social justice issue related to the campus in order to fulfill the assignment, tell them the location of the presentations, and let them know that they will need to invite audience members. The suggested time limit for presentations is 15 to 18 minutes, with another 5 minutes for audience questions.

We encourage you to incorporate self-reflection opportunities for each student; this can be accomplished in a journal or essay and can be done weekly or at the end of the unit. Invite students to reflect on their individual performance in regards to team meetings, participation and contribution of ideas, and collaboration. Additionally, students should provide weekly peer evaluations, which provide a reflection of the team members' participation within group meetings, contributions of ideas, and overall group communication.

Divide the class into groups of four to five members. We suggest dividing into groups in whatever way that best fits the personalities and needs of each student individually, as well as each group as a whole. Have each group decide on a leader who will act as a contact person, prepare weekly agendas, and facilitate weekly meetings. Additionally, another group member may act as recorder to submit detailed minutes to their group members and for a grade. To stay informed regarding each group's progress, agendas and minutes should be turned in weekly. While the leader and recorder have assigned roles, all group members will perform various tasks each week, such as being assigned research, developing visual aids, outlining, and so forth. If teaching an introduction to communication course, instructors will most likely have to provide more guidance to ensure that students are collaboratively making and meeting team goals, schedules, and deadlines. After establishing small groups, give 20 to 25 minutes of class time for groups to brainstorm topics. Finally, instruct the groups that they must compose a memo to send to key decision makers on campus, explaining their issue and inviting them to the presentation. The memo draft is due to the instructor during Week 2.

WEEK 2: WORK GROUPS

Week 2 is for research and publicity. At the beginning of the week, lead a discussion on how to research the topic using library databases and personal interviews with campus stakeholders. Each group is required to have a minimum of 10 audience members (who are not enrolled in the class) at the symposium. Classroom discussion should focus on practical tips for publicizing events on a college campus, such as utilizing social media, campus newspapers, campus boards and marquees. Finally, groups should submit the first draft of the memo for instructor feedback. Students are to revise the memo for Week 3.

WEEK 3: ORGANIZATION

The purpose of Week 3 is to organize the presentation. Groups are asked to choose individual roles for their presentations and to create a group outline. There are four roles to fulfill on a symposium panel. The moderator introduces the topic and presenters, provides a clear conclusion, and fields questions from the audience. After the introduction by the moderator, a panelist should describe the group's identified problem on campus. The next speaker should discuss up to five potential solutions. The final speaker should address the group's best solution and address an action plan to resolve the problem, which should be grounded in research, benefit and incorporate multiple stakeholders, and do more than merely suggest that administrators fix the problem. If there are more than four members in a group, double up the speakers on one or more of the sections. The moderator finishes the symposium by opening the floor for questions. The instructor should stress the importance of civic discourse during Q&A. Memos are generally of high quality by Week 3 and are ready to distribute to key decision makers.

WEEK 4: REHEARSAL AND ASSESSMENT

Tie up loose ends during Week 4. Groups should have detailed outlines and be prepared to rehearse during class to receive peer and instructor feedback. In class, discuss audience expectations and grading criteria. This assignment should be assessed for both the process of teamwork and the product of a public performance. While many rubrics exist to evaluate the symposium, such as the Valid Assessment of Learning in Undergraduate Education (VALUE, 2014) rubrics from the Association of American Colleges & Universities (AAC&U), original rubrics can be created to assess overall group work, presentation organization, critical thinking, and/or delivery.

WEEK 5: PRESENTATIONS

Week 5 showcases the public presentations. Each symposium takes 20 to 23 minutes. Allow for 10-minute breaks between presentations in order to permit the audiences to move in and out and for panelists to get set up. All symposia can take place during one long class period or could be spread out over multiple class times.

REFLEXIVE APPRAISAL

The public symposium unit is a helpful way to engage learners in articulating their concerns for social justice on their campuses in a public setting. It provides an opportunity for students to use skills learned from their communication classes to voice and discuss their ideas with stakeholders, concerned citizens, and decision makers. It makes it clear to them that they do have voice in the spaces in which they live, work, and go to school.

Of course, there are potential pitfalls with any assignment. Five weeks is a long time for students to collaboratively focus on one assignment. They may grow frustrated with each other, the people they depend on for interviews, and the requirements. Additionally, students may find it difficult to approach topics outside of their comfort zones. It is important to pay close attention to the mood of the students; this can be done through face-to-face and mediated interactions as well as weekly journals.

Some of the students may experience communication apprehension and experience anxiety when it comes to speaking in public. They will need opportunities to discuss strategies for how to reduce public speaking anxiety before the formal public presentation. Outside consultation from a communication resource center should be promoted if available. A final concern is that hostile audience members may challenge students during the Q&A section of their symposium. Prepare students for a variety of questions and perspectives from the audience and give them tips for how to engage in civic discourse in relation to the topic.

REFERENCES

Cragan, J. F., Kash, C. R., & Wright, D. W. (2009). *Communication in small groups: Theory, process, and skills* (7th ed.). Boston, MA: Wadsworth Cengage.

Englebert, I. N., & Wynn, D. R. (2012). *Working in groups* (6th ed). Boston, MA: Allyn & Bacon.

Fassett, D. L., & Warren, J. T. (2007). *Critical communication pedagogy*. Thousand Oaks, CA: Sage Publications.

NCA. (2015). *Drawing learning outcomes in communication into meaningful practice.* The National Communication Association's Learning Outcomes in Communication Project. Retrieved from https://www.natcom.org/sites/default/files/publications/LOC_2_Drawing_Learning_Outcomes_in_Communication.pdf

VALUE. (2014). *Rubric development project.* Association of American Colleges & Universities. Retrieved from http://www.aacu.org/value/rubrics.

ACTIVITY 9

INCLUSIVE LANGUAGE PUBLIC SERVICE ANNOUNCEMENTS

LELAND G. SPENCER

RATIONALE

Many introductory communication courses include units or lessons about verbal communication, and textbooks for such courses explicitly discuss examples of harmful language such as sexist, racist, or homophobic language, and encourage students to avoid using such harmful language. While I find these lessons important, I also worry that a focus on avoiding harmful language may contribute to an ongoing perception that college and university campuses promote "political correctness" and a corresponding oversensitivity among students. In contradistinction to that now-tired refrain, I suggest that political correctness has a basis in fear: the fear of offending someone or saying something wrong. Instead, this activity encourages students to embrace inclusive language as part of an overall ethic of respect and care for human dignity. Ethical communicators use inclusive language and avoid harmful language not because we fear offending someone, but because we recognize and celebrate the inherent worth of every person (Foss & Griffin, 1995; Spencer, 2013), and we want to speak or write in a way that acknowledges the humanity of others. These aims comport with the larger goals of social justice pedagogy to the degree that language often represents, sustains, and forwards hegemonic systems of oppression and injustice (Spencer, 2015a). I understand actively and intentionally embracing inclusive language as a necessary step in the process of creating "a more humanizing and humane world," a core objective of critical communication pedagogy (Warren & Fassett, 2010, p. 290).

COURSE(S):

Introduction to Communication; Public Speaking; Gender and Communication

OBJECTIVE(S) (NCA, 2015):

After completing this activity, students should be able to:

- critically analyze messages with attention to the inclusiveness of their language,
- apply ethical communication principles and practices to language use, and
- use communication to embrace difference by speaking in ways that celebrate diversity.

ACTIVITY

PREPARATION

1. (Optional) Assign students to read West and Turner's (2012) or Wood's (2011) textbook chapter about verbal communication.
2. Use a classroom with audiovisual capabilities or arrange for a media cart.
3. Cue the YouTube videos cited below before class, clearing ads as necessary.
4. Prepare pieces of paper or notecards with examples of harmful language.

DESCRIPTION

This activity asks students to work in groups to develop a public service announcement for the class to explain why a given example of harmful language is problematic, and to offer alternatives to communicate the intended idea more inclusively. Before class, students read the textbook chapter about verbal communication (depending on the class, West & Turner [2012] or Wood [2011]). I begin class with a lecture about the difference between inclusive language and political correctness by asking students how they define "political correctness." Student answers always center on making sure no one will be offended by what they say. I trace the theme of fear in students' definitions of political correctness, and then I explain why I find inclusive language a more positive and affirmative approach. Then I work through several examples of problematic language, engaging students in discussion and conversation about the implications of each type of harmful language and the more inclusive alternatives. For instance, we talk about sexist language including the male generic ("Someone left his book last week"), language that erases the existence and experience of women ("I now pronounce you man and wife"), and the non-parallelism of diminutive suffixes ("waiter vs. waitress") and racist language such as spotlighting or marked language ("Dr. Keller is a good Black dentist") and using dark or black as a synonym for bad ("blacklisting" or even the unfortunate tendency of interpersonal textbooks to classify lying or infidelity as "the dark side" of interpersonal communication). Along the way, we discuss more inclusive alternatives to most types of harmful language.

After the discussion, I tell the students they will have an opportunity to apply what we talked about by creating a public service announcement for the class. I explain that I have a few phrases with examples of problematic language, and I ask the students to work in groups to explain the harmfulness of the problematic language, including the language's implications, and then offer some alternative or inclusive ways to change the language presented.

Before I give the groups their examples of problematic language, I show them two or three YouTube clips with public service announcements about language, including the Gay, Lesbian, and Straight Education Network's public service announcement featuring Wanda Sykes on "That's so Gay" (GLSEN, 2008), the cast of *Glee* on the "r-word" (retarded; Spread the Word, 2011), and Race Forward's (2015) charge to "Drop the 'I' Word" (illegal, in reference to immigrants). We briefly discuss and critique the videos, focusing on what we learned from the videos and how the videos could improve; none of the videos, for instance, give clear alternatives to the language they suggest we drop. I next give students time to work in their groups. I give each group a sentence, such as, "Anne doesn't work. She's just a housewife" or "Hey, Alberto. I like your jeans. No homo, though!" or "Why are you so upset? Just man up!"

While students work, I walk around the room and eavesdrop on conversations, jumping in when students feel confused or need some guidance. For example, one of the problem sentences reads, "Ron can't come out tonight because he has to babysit his son." Some groups struggle to identify the problem in this sentence, so I ask probing questions such as, "How would this sentence sound different if we used a woman's name instead?" If they did not get it before, students immediately realize the inappropriateness of "babysit" in that sentence; when a man takes care of his child, we call it parenting, not babysitting. After I get a sense that students have finished preparing, I invite groups to take turns presenting to the class.

DEBRIEFING

Most groups present short performances or simply discuss their phrase, its problematic implications, and some alternatives. I allow a minute or two for questions or discussion before the next group presents. To assess the activity, I use the two questions I give each group along with the problematic phrase on the notecard: What are the implications of this phrase? And what alternatives might we use to communicate the same idea in a way that reflects respect for human dignity? I expect the groups to address these two questions in their presentation, and class discussion after each presentation affords an opportunity to fill in the gaps for anything the groups miss.

REFLEXIVE APPRAISAL

Instructors who wish to adapt this activity into a graded project could allow for out-of-class preparation time and require a creative video or a longer presentation from each group. I always use it as a class activity for which students receive participation points. As such, some groups take it less seriously or fail to engage as fully. With any class activity, students perform with a range of success. In some cases I have needed to do more prompting and filling in when a group finishes than in other cases. Instructors may also wish to supplement with textbook material about language, such as including an explicit discussion about gender identity and gendered pronoun use (see Adams, 2015; Spencer, 2015b) or the importance of person-first language when talking or writing about persons with disabilities (Isgro, 2015).

For all the benefits of this activity, it sometimes comes with challenges. Because I have always used this activity in more politically conservative climates, students sometimes object to the video about the word "illegal" and want to start a debate about immigration policy. Depending on time, I sometimes cut that video and only show the other two videos, which I have found keeps the activity more focused. Student resistance might also come in the form of students who use harmful language in class, such as slurs about sexual orientation. This activity allows instructors to use those moments as chances to ask students to think about the implications of using such language and to reflect on how those language choices might communicate disrespect or disregard for other people. By focusing on human dignity, instructors link the issue of language to social justice, something broader than the individualism at the heart of movements for political correctness.

REFERENCES

Adams, M. A. (2015). Traversing the transcape: A brief historical etymology of trans* terminology. In L. G. Spencer & J. Capuzza (Eds.), *Transgender communication studies: Histories, trends, and trajectories* (pp. 173–185). Lanham, MD: Lexington.

GLSEN. (2008). That's so gay – Wanda Sykes [Video file]. Retrieved from https://www.youtube.com/watch?v=sWS0GVOQPs0.

Isgro, K. (2015). From a caretaker's perspective: Mothers of children with Down syndrome as advocates. *Women & Language*, 38(1), 63–82.

Foss, S. K., & Griffin, C. L. (1995). Beyond persuasion: A proposal for an invitational rhetoric. *Communication Monographs,* 62(1), 2–18. doi:10.1080/03637759509376345

NCA. (2015). *Drawing learning outcomes in communication into meaningful practice.* The National Communication Association's Learning Outcomes in Communication Project. Retrieved from https://www.natcom.org/sites/default/files/publications/LOC_2_Drawing_Learning_Outcomes_in_Communication.pdf

Race Forward. (2015). Why we should drop the I-word [Video file]. Retrieved from https://www.youtube.com/watch?list=PL4ruTyc9FHOXIiw7XW1kF424I4wRPGRo8&v=K4KObY2tqe4.

Spencer, L. G. (2013). Presiding Bishop Katharine Jefferts Schori and possibilities for a progressive civility. *Southern Communication Journal*, 78(5), 447–465. http://doi.org/10.1080/1041794X.2013.847480

Spencer, L. G. (2015a). Engaging undergraduates in feminist classrooms: An exploration of professors' practices. *Equity & Excellence in Education*, 48(2), 195–211. http://doi.org/10.1080/10665684.2015.1022909

Spencer, L. G. (2015b). Introduction: Centering transgender studies and gender identity in communication scholarship. In L. G. Spencer & J. Capuzza (Eds.), *Transgender communication studies: Histories, trends, and trajectories* (pp. ix–xxii). Lanham, MD: Lexington.

Spread the Word to End the Word. (2011). Not acceptable – R-word PSA [Video file]. Retrieved from https://www.youtube.com/watch?v=6y5hLlXnAOQ.

Warren, J. T., & Fassett, D. L. (2010). Critical communication pedagogy: Reframing the field. In D. L. Fassett & J. T. Warren (Eds.), *The SAGE handbook of communication and instruction* (pp. 283–291). Thousand Oaks, CA: Sage Publications.

West, R., & Turner, L. H. (2012). *IPC*. Boston, MA: Wadsworth.

Wood, J. T. (2011). *Gendered lives: Communication, gender, and culture* (9th ed.). Boston, MA: Wadsworth.

ACTIVITY 10

FAIR TRADE ADVOCACY: A CASE STUDY FOR STUDENT INVOLVEMENT ON CAMPUS

BRADLEY WOLFE

RATIONALE

This activity is designed to help students see fair trade as a communicative relationship between consumers and producers. Fairtrade International (2011) defines fair trade as "an alternative approach to conventional trade and is based on a partnership between producers and consumers" (para. 1). Fair trade creates social justice in the alternative trade system by empowering producers to set the prices for their goods at a living wage through the use of communicative symbols in branding. Through cooperative social and economic action, fair trade producers communicate to consumers the conditions of production. Consumers communicate how important social justice is to them by purchasing fair trade products, which may cost more than market prices for goods of equal quality. More than just a label on the side of a product we buy, fair trade is reframed as a relationship encompassing the localities of production and consumption within a shared, global community of social justice. This lesson builds on the ideals of social justice educator Paulo Freire. Specifically, the activities involved utilize his see-judge-act approach to social justice education (Gibson, 1999). The lesson invites students to see consumer purchases as situated within the global landscape of production. Students are better positioned to understand their consumer choices as judgments about that landscape and their role in it. Those judgments become actions in the form of actual purchases students make.

Fassett and Warren (2007) applied Freire's work to communication pedagogy. Their critical communication pedagogy places structural critiques of social communicative acts in a meaningful context. In the lesson, fair trade as a communicative act introduces students to the societal structures that can unite consumer consciousness with the livelihood of the producers in the global south. Through fair trade purchases, consumers engage in metaphorical dialogue with the foreign producers. As part of the introduction to communication course, the lesson facilitates an integration of social justice, communication pedagogy, and community interaction. Students will engage communication concepts on a practical level. Often students are enrolled in the courses not to learn how to be better communicators, but rather to fill a general education requirement. Critical communication pedagogy elevates the value of their learning throughout the semester through practical activities that engage the local community.

COURSE(S):

Introduction to Communication; Communication, Community, and Change

OBJECTIVE(S) (NCA, 2015):

When completing this activity, students should be able to:

- evaluate ethical elements of the communicative process of fair trade,
- articulate personal beliefs about their ability to communicate ethically with producers, and
- apply communication theories, perspectives, principles, and concepts to navigate power differences in an organizational structure.

ACTIVITY

Students will begin with a reading about how a successful advocacy campaign was established and sustained on a college campus. The reading and following discussion will help students see how they can use their communication skills to impact social justice efforts on their own campus and in the community. The students will learn more about how fair trade creates a socially just relationship between producers and consumers by watching a TEDx Talk video about fair trade (Conard, 2015).

Instructors will then have the opportunity to challenge their students to apply their communication skills to learn about local fair trade efforts.

Students start by reading Chapter Six, A Fair Trade University, in *Fair Trade from the Ground Up: New Markets for Social Justice* by April Linton (2012). The reading can be completed before class for 50-minute sessions, or during class for 75-minute sessions. The chapter describes how a group of students at the University of California—San Diego successfully convinced administrators and many vendors on campus to sell fair trade products as the default offering. Stories are shared within the case study to bring to life the challenges in growing the campaign from a handful of students asking for change to the university implementing fair trade as policy.

Once students have the opportunity to read the chapter, have them form small groups for discussion. Give each group the following discussion questions to consider in conversation for 15 minutes:

1. How did the group of students use communication to start the fair trade campaign? How did they organize themselves to produce the greatest impact with their communication?
2. What was One Earth One Justice's primary purpose? Why did the group take on a fair trade campaign on their campus?
3. In their initial effort, which stakeholders were the group able to convince to join the fair trade movement? How were they able to successfully communicate their desires to those groups?
4. Why was the administration reluctant to join the group of advocates? What other objections did stakeholders have to adopting fair trade standards?
5. What communication strategies did the group use to overcome the objections? What projects did their fair trade campaign include?
6. What can we take away from their efforts? How can we implement the communication tools they used to create a successful campaign on our own campus?

Once the groups have discussed these questions, have them report back to the whole class. One question at a time, have each group share the insight gained from the discussion. Start with a different group on each question before opening the conversation to the whole class. Rotating which group answers first ensures every group shares at least once about what they discussed. For the last question, write on the board what communication strategies the students took away from the chapter. Make sure to emphasize how the tools can be used in a variety of advocacy campaigns besides just fair trade.

Before showing the video, transition the class by acknowledging how students can make a difference without starting a long-term advocacy campaign. "Fair Trade: A Just World Starts with You" (Conard, 2015) explains smaller actions everyone can take to align their social values with their consumer purchases. Conard (2015) connects the small purchases we buy every day to the communicative connection established between producers and consumers. Now, show the 10-minute video to the class.

Following the video, discuss with the class what fair trade products are sold on campus and in the local community. Typically, many of the students may not know the opportunities to support fair trade in their own community. Challenge them to find out where fair trade products may be purchased. Ask students to raise their hands if they are willing to find at least one business or location on campus that offers a fair trade option within the next week. Out of those students, ask who is willing to make a fair trade purchase and bring it back to class for the next week.

DEBRIEFING

A variation on challenging students to raise their hand is to assign a fair trade resource hunt as homework. Beforehand, find five to seven locations on campus and/or near campus that sell fair trade products. Instruct students to visit each location within a week's time to find out what specific products they offer. Students should record their findings in a notebook or by taking a picture with a cell phone. In order to build off the scavenger hunt, assign a one-to-two-page essay using the following questions regarding the opportunities in the community for socially just communication with producers:

1. Is fair trade accepted within mainstream capitalism? Why or why not?
2. What barriers prevent fair trade purchasing opportunities from being readily available in the community?
3. How might some of the strategies you learned from the case study and TEDx Talk be applied in other areas of your life, work, and community?

REFLEXIVE APPRAISAL

While the lesson has critical pedagogical value in bringing to light how students can become actively involved in global social justice issues, instructors should recognize the limits of fair trade as a tool to alleviate systemic poverty. Supporting fair trade through consumer engagement will not, in and of itself, put to rest the societal structure that creates sectors of abundant wealth and admonished poverty. Fair trade's limited reach does allow consumers to send messages of acknowledgement and respect for the effort put into producing the consumed goods. Communication should be at the heart of the lesson to acknowledge the current reach of the fair trade movement. Specifically, communication allows students to see the fair trade producers through the lens of an interpersonal partnership based on equality. The partnership created between the producers and consumers is that of two equals with dignity and respect between them (Fairtrade International, 2011). Fair trade has not been developed merely to rid consumers of guilt (another capitalist discourse) or to create new avenues for charitable donations. Instructors need to emphasize the communicative relationship created through fair trade processes.

REFERENCES

Conard, B. (2015, April 22). Benjamin Conard: Fair trade: A just world starts with you [Video file]. Retrieved from https://www.youtube.com/watch?v=xT6TQSxlDOY.

Fairtrade International. (2011). *What is fair trade?* Retrieved from the Fairtrade Labelling Organizations International website: http://www.fairtrade.net/what-is-fairtrade.html.

Fassett, D. L., & Warren, J. T. (2007). *Critical communication pedagogy.* Thousand Oaks, CA: Sage Publications.

Gibson, R. (1999). Paulo Freire and pedagogy for social justice. *Theory & Research in Social Education, 27*(2), 129–159.

Linton, A. (2012). *Fair trade from the ground up: New markets for social justice.* Seattle, WA: University of Washington Press.

NCA. (2015). *Drawing learning outcomes in communication into meaningful practice.* The National Communication Association's Learning Outcomes in Communication Project. Retrieved from https://www.natcom.org/sites/default/files/publications/LOC_2_Drawing_Learning_Outcomes_in_Communication.pdf

TEACHING CRITICAL INQUIRY AND
SOCIALLY JUST COMMUNICATION

DANIELLE M. DE LA MARE

RATIONALE

Because newer college students do not usually have a frame of reference for understanding a critical perspective, they're often confused after having read about the topic in the first chapter of Fassett and Warren's (2015) *Communication: A Critical/Cultural Introduction*. This activity not only illustrations to students, through an extended example, what a critical perspective entails, it also asks them to apply a critical perspective to their own educational experiences, which, as Fassett and Warren (2007) explain, lies at the heart of critical communication pedagogy: where inquiry "is about identity, about subjectivity, about who we are as people, people who are invested and produced in the process of education" (p. 71). This activity, then, invites students to expand their current perceptions by deconstructing one way our educational system may actually harm and strip people of voice and opportunity; encourages them to discuss their own "miseducation"; and attempts to empower them by utilizing modes of communication toward more socially just ends.

COURSES:

Introductory Communication Course

OBJECTIVE(S):

- Identify meanings embedded in messages.
- Identify ethical perspectives.
- Propose solutions for (un)ethical communication.
- Empower individuals to promote human rights, human dignity, and human freedom.

ACTIVITY

SET UP

Prior to class, the instructor should find a copy of the article "A curriculum of aloha? Colonialism and tourism in Hawaii's elementary textbooks" by Julie Kaomea (2000) and be ready to project (e.g., with PowerPoint) the images used on pages 326–330 in class. Kaomea is a critical education scholar who has done extensive research on Native Hawaiian Studies as it has been implemented in Hawaii's public schools. The images shown on these pages illustrate the similarities between the textbooks being used in elementary schools and the images used in Hawaii's tourist industry—images that have been intimately shaped by Hawaii's colonialist history.

FIRST STEP

The instructor tells students that in the 1970s Hawaii revised their state constitution to ensure all public school students were educated about Native Hawaiian culture, history, and language. The instructor should emphasize the progressive nature of this law and do a lot of cheerleading about how noble, responsible, and respectful it is. I tell students how impressed I was when I first heard about Hawaii's mandate and discuss how much I wish we were as progressive in Michigan. I write on the board, "GREAT! Go Hawaii!" This is reflective of my teaching style and personality. Instructors should feel free to emphasize the positive aspects of this mandate in whatever way feels appropriate with their specific classroom community, including discussing the benefits of such a policy. This is the "set up."

SECOND STEP

Tell students you found some research about how Hawaiian Studies has been implemented. Tell them you want to share three pieces of evidence with them. First, show them the postcard images on pages 327–330 and tell them that each slide juxtaposes an image from a postcard next to a picture in a commonly used Hawaiian Studies textbook. I usually allow students to silently look at each photo.

THIRD STEP

Tell students these images come from a textbook called *Hawaii: The Aloha State*. Tell them too that Kaomea found dozens of other books by the same name, but that these other books were *not* textbooks. Ask them what type of books might be titled *Hawaii: The Aloha State*. Students almost immediately say they are tourist guidebooks, which is true. To sustain interest, show them the images on page 326, where Kaomea juxtaposes a picture of the textbook cover next to a picture of a Hawaiian travel guidebook of the same name. Comment about how strange it is that these books have the same name.

Continue to heighten students' concerns by reading aloud a paragraph from Kaomea's (2000) research on page 338 (toward the bottom of the page), where she describes a fourth-grade activity used in the Hawaiian studies curriculum: an activity that requires elementary students to make travel arrangements for foreigners visiting Hawaii. Again, comment about the strangeness of this activity for teaching Native Hawaiian Studies.

FOURTH STEP

At this point, the instructor has walked students through critical inquiry and slowly peeled back various layers of information. Remind students that our original assessment of the Native Hawaiian Studies curriculum was "GREAT! Go Hawaii!" Ask them why any of this new information should matter and why we should care about Kaomea's research. To these questions, students become eager to offer their (very critical) perspectives. They say things like, "This isn't an education!" Others might say that it ignores Native Hawaiian perspectives or that it denies student voice. At this point, allow them to guide the discussion: Allow them to ask their critical questions, make their critical assessments, discuss the connections they're making to the education they have received, and freely express their anger and sadness about the situation.

Tell them they'll now think more deeply about communication and public advocacy. Divide the class in half. Tell the students on one side of the classroom to imagine that they're teachers in Hawaii and have recently become concerned about the Hawaiian Studies curriculum they're being asked to teach. Have them work in small groups of two to three to think of ways they might communicate their concerns to others. Tell the students on the other side of the classroom to imagine they're parents of a school-aged child and they've become concerned after looking over her or his textbook. Again, ask them to get in groups of two to three and explore what a responsible parent might do communicatively. Give students five to ten minutes to talk to each other.

DEBRIEFING

When students return to the large group discussion, record their answers on the board (e.g., talk to the principal, form a group of like-minded parents). Once the master list has been constructed, tell them these are all forms of public advocacy. Ask them why public advocacy is important in this scenario (the benefits), what the consequences or risks might be, and whether they believe the benefits outweigh the risks. The last question generates dynamic discussion. End the discussion by asking students about a specific local issue that may require critical analysis and public advocacy. This allows students to begin thinking about their own public advocacy projects, which I require at the end of the semester.

REFLEXIVE APPRAISAL

Because this activity generates energetic discussion, engages students deeply, and illustrates for them the contours of critical inquiry, public advocacy, and social justice, it serves as a wonderful semester kick-off for the second or third day of class. The activity builds a strong foundation that gives students clarity about the social justice goals of the course and attempts to empower them to practice critical inquiry in all parts of their lives. Most importantly, I consciously and caringly try to design the course, daily lesson plans, and student assignments to engage students in this practice from a variety of culturally inclusive and dialogically relational ways.

One of biggest challenges—perhaps the biggest challenge—for me as a teacher of social justice is that I will never have enough time and space to do everything that *should* be done. This activity was born out of need and pressure: I needed to find a way to teach students, in a concrete manner, the realities of critical inquiry, and I felt pressure because our class meeting was fast approaching. But, after submitting my initial draft of this piece, the authors of this textbook asked me what it means (to me) to use the oppression of Native Hawaiians as simply a "teaching tool." They didn't require I explore the issue, but in the spirit of reflexive practice, they asked the question, which I could choose to either explore or not explore here. As a critical communication pedagogue who strives to be honest and collaborative, I will admit that I've asked this question of myself in fleeting moments, but I've never taken it seriously enough to answer it. Today, after scanning my emotions and realizing (and owning this realization) that I feel ambivalence and discomfort having decided to write this final paragraph, I know only one thing: I'm now committed to exploring this question with my students. Together, in community, we will talk about the ethical implications and decide what we, as a class collective, should do going forward.

REFERENCES

Fassett, D. L., & Warren, J. T. (2007). *Critical communication pedagogy*. Thousand Oaks, CA: Sage Publications.

Kaomea, J. (2000). A curriculum of Aloha? Colonialism and tourism in Hawai'i's elementary textbooks. *Curriculum Inquiry, 30*(3), 319–344.

Warren, J. T., & Fassett, D. L. (2015). *Communication: A critical/cultural introduction* (2nd ed.). Thousand Oaks, CA: Sage Publications.

ACTIVITY 12

CONSTRUCTING CRITICAL CONNECTIONS, CHALLENGING KINDERGARTEN ASSUMPTIONS, AND ENGAGING RADICAL REFLEXIVITY IN COMMUNICATION COURSES

LISA HANASONO

RATIONALE

Critical communication pedagogy provides critical- and social justice–oriented educators a framework that challenges students to interrogate and challenge everyday assumptions, values, and beliefs that are espoused in dominant discourses (Allen, 2011; Fassett & Warren, 2007). In the United States, kindergarten often indoctrinates students to accept dominant ideologies about teaching, learning, and socialization practices in school settings. From language acquisition skills (e.g., learning the alphabet and expanding students' vocabularies) and procedural knowledge (e.g., how to ask permission for a bathroom break) to social interaction skills (e.g., sharing with friends and obeying the teacher), schools expect students to assimilate into their educational institutions. Unfortunately, many of the lessons that students learn in school become "taken for granted" knowledge that is rarely questioned or contested.

Universities and colleges across the nation are committed to teaching students how to think critically and make connections between theory and praxis (AAUP, 2011). This commitment to critical thinking is underscored in the communication discipline; for example, the National Communication Association's (NCA, 2015) fifth recommended learning outcome states that students should be able to "critically analyze messages" (p. 7). Burman (2000) explains that critical thinking requires individuals to question widely accepted theories, suspend personal biases and preconceptions, and evaluate information. Unfortunately, many students struggle to identify values and assumptions that are embedded in research articles, class processes, and the ways in which they engage with others in everyday life. Inspired by Robert Fulghum's (1986) book, *All I Really Need to Know I Learned in Kindergarten*, this activity teaches students how to identify, question, and evaluate everyday assumptions. Moreover, this activity helps students make connections between critical thinking and communication.

COURSES:

Introduction to Communication; Public Speaking; Rhetorical Criticism; Intercultural Communication

OBJECTIVE(S) (NCA, 2015):

By completing this activity, students should be able to:

- identify, analyze, and critically evaluate normative everyday assumptions,
- differentiate value and descriptive assumptions, and
- evaluate scholarly assumptions in academic articles.

ACTIVITY

To begin, instructors should inform students that they will be completing an activity that challenges them to identify their values and evaluate everyday assumptions. Browne and Keeley (2012) define values as "the unstated ideas that people see as worthwhile. They provide standards of conduct by which we measure the quality of human behavior" (p. 57). Examples of values include autonomy, justice, equality, and harmony. Browne and Keeley (2012) define an assumption as "a belief, usually unstated, that is taken for granted and supports explicit reasoning" (p. 58). They explain that people hold two types of assumptions: value and descriptive. *Value assumptions* are "an implicit preference for one value over another in a particular context" (p. 59); they reflect our beliefs about the ways that the world should operate.

On the other hand, *descriptive assumptions* focus on "the way the world *was, is, or will be*" (Browne & Keeley, 2012, p. 65). For example, some people may hold a value assumption that "honesty is the best policy." These individuals maintain a high regard for openness and full disclosure; they believe that people should be honest with each other. However, the same people may believe that a political candidate is not trustworthy due to an established record of broken promises. In this case, their value assumptions underscore the desirability of honest behaviors, while their descriptive assumptions indicate an expectation of deceptive behaviors from political candidates.

Instructors may wish to explain why students must be able to identify, analyze, and critique value and description assumptions (e.g., it will help them analyze their own and others' arguments, avoid fallacious reasoning, and allow for more informed decision-making processes). If desired, instructors can provide examples of false assumptions that have been held by historical figures (e.g., Ptolemy's model that placed Earth in the center of our universe or the erroneous belief that Earth was flat).

Next, instructors should explain that people operate on everyday assumptions. We learned many of these assumptions during the socialization process involved in our childhoods. Instructors should introduce Fulghum's (1986) notion that "all [we] need to know [we] learned in kindergarten." Fulghum argues that some of the most important lessons are taught in kindergarten—not in high school or higher education. In general, the lessons that we learn in kindergarten act as a set of foundational assumptions in the ways we see the world and how we interact with others. Although many of these lessons have merit, we rarely think critically about them. This activity will challenge students to question, evaluate, and consider the implications of the assumptions we formed in kindergarten. Furthermore, this activity gives students an opportunity to think more critically about the values and assumptions made by communication researchers and educators.

IMPLEMENTATION

Instructors should invite students to organize themselves into small groups (i.e., 3 to 5 students). Each group will receive one of the Fulghum's (1986) lessons:

1. Share everything.
2. Don't take things that aren't yours.

3. Warm cookies and milk are good for you.
4. Take a nap every afternoon.
5. Clean up your own mess.
6. Play fair.
7. Live a balanced life.

Working in their groups, students should first identify the assumption (e.g., "people should treat others the way that they would like to be treated") and discuss what types of values are needed for a person to hold that assumption. Second, students should assess the assumption by identifying its underlying values, implications (e.g., How might this assumption affect the ways that we think, behave, or interact with others?), strengths (e.g., Why might this assumption be helpful?), and limitations (e.g., Why might this assumption be problematic?). Finally, students should craft a conclusion about the assumption (i.e., after considering the merits and limitations of the assumption—and alternative assumptions—to what extent do students recommend the original assumption?).

DEBRIEFING

After approximately 5 to 10 minutes, allow each group of students to present its findings. Then, facilitate a discussion session to help students critically reflect on the activity. Here are some sample questions:

1. In this activity, you identified and evaluated some everyday assumptions that are popular in the United States. Why is it important to question our own and popular public assumptions?
2. Many assumptions are contextualized through a specific culture. Think about *your* cultural background. What are some common assumptions held by your cultures? What are the implications of these assumptions?
3. What should you do when you discover that another person has made an erroneous cultural assumption?
4. In this activity, you focused on everyday assumptions. However, it is important to note that communication researchers, educators, and scholars make assertions and draw conclusions that are based on sets of assumptions. How

can you identify scholarly assumptions? When should you challenge them? How should you challenge them?

5. Think of a recent class reading (or presentation). What assumptions did the author (or presenter) make? How did it affect their communication? Do you agree with their assumptions? Why or why not?

REFLEXIVE APPRAISALS

Critical communication pedagogy "advocates a social justice orientation for transforming oppressive educational institutions into sites of emancipation and equality ... [and] examines impacts of dominant ideologies on teaching and learning" (Allen, 2011, p. 104). Guided by principles of critical communication pedagogy, this activity has been particularly successful because it (a) challenges students to critically reflect and question every day assumptions, (b) encourages them to transfer their critical thinking skills to identify and evaluate meaningful assumptions that are held by communication scholars, and (c) has the potential to awaken in students a desire to question existing codes and conventions. From lessons learned in kindergarten to scholarly arguments in published articles, students learn how value and descriptive assumptions guide the logic of dominant educational discourses. In past semesters, my students have thoroughly enjoyed this activity.

Many admitted that they had never thought critically about the everyday lessons they learned in kindergarten and throughout their childhood; this activity helped them reflect on their primary and secondary educational experiences in a new light. Moreover, some of my students indicated that the activity challenged them to reengage with their college coursework and readings. Instead of focusing primarily on memorizing vocabulary words or summarizing key arguments in an article, students began to interrogate the underlying assumptions of their texts. Despite this activity's merits, several potential pitfalls exist. First, some students struggle initially to identify and articulate the statements' assumptions. Instructors can help students avoid this pitfall by working through an example with the class before the groups tackle the activity. Second, students tend to have a more difficult time identifying key assumptions from college-level readings (e.g., research studies or communication scholarship) than Fulghum's (1986) statements. Instructors can provide an example or use guiding, open-ended questions to help students initially uncover and identify key assumptions from their readings.

While this activity could address the educational needs of students from many different disciplines, it is particularly applicable for communication courses, given its focus on identifying and critiquing assumptions that underpin dominant discourses. In addition to being able to understand and use scholarly theories, principles, and concepts, the National Communication Association (NCA, 2015) indicates that it is imperative for communication students to be able to "critically analyze messages" and "utilize communication to embrace difference" (p. 7). By empowering students with the tools to identify, analyze, and assess everyday, taken-for-granted assumptions, this activity invites students to think more reflexively about messages that reinforce oppressive, dominant ideologies.

REFERENCES

AAUP. (2011). *Campaign for the future of higher ed principles.* Retrieved from http://www.aaup.org/node/207

Allen, B. J. (2011). *Difference matters: Communicating social identity* (2nd ed.). Long Grove, IL: Waveland Press.

Browne, M. N., & Keeley, S. M. (2012). *Asking the right questions: A guide to critical thinking.* Boston, MA: Pearson.

Burman, S. (2000). Critical thinking: Its application to substance abuse education and practice. *Journal of Teaching in Social Work, 20,* 155–171. doi: 10.1300/J067v20n03_11

Fassett, D. L., & Warren, J. T. (2007). *Critical communication pedagogy.* Thousand Oaks, CA: Sage Publications.

Fulghum, R. (1986). *All I really need to know I learned in kindergarten.* New York, NY: Ballantine Books.

NCA. (2015). *Drawing learning outcomes in communication into meaningful practice.* The National Communication Association's Learning Outcomes in Communication Project. Retrieved from https://www.natcom.org/sites/default/files/publications/LOC_2_Drawing_Learning_Outcomes_in_Communication.pdf

---

ACTIVITY 13

RIDING ALONG WITH RACISM: USING *COPS* TO TEACH MEDIA REPRESENTATION

MATT FOY

RATIONALE

Understanding the constitutive nature of popular culture and the commercial mass media is a crucial outcome in any introductory communication course. As Warren and Fassett (2015) write in their introductory course textbook, "Like fish immersed in water, we swim constantly through media, which develop and shape our perceptions, goals, desires, and beliefs" (p. 211). And though 21st-century technological developments have empowered voices on the margins to reach larger audiences than in prior eras, the mediated landscape of the United States remains dominated by a small oligarchy of multinational for-profit corporations (see Bagdikian, 2004) that promote conservative values such as neoliberalism, capitalism, and state-sponsored violence as social corrective. Commercial media producers functionally crystalize these destructive mythologies through mediated representation in pleasing narrative form (see Barthes, 1972). Thus, critical media literacy is a vital goal for a communication course interested in the pursuit of social justice, for the capacity to resist and deconstruct oppressive discourses embedded in cultural texts is a skill that can be developed through practice and access to a heuristic vocabulary for everyday criticism.

One example of a pervasive mediated text that serves as a conduit for practicing media literacy is the television show *COPS*. Currently in its 28th season, *COPS* is among the longest-running representatives of the reality television genre. Each episode features a series of short, self-contained, documentary-style clips of law enforcement officers pursuing and successfully arresting persons in the act of breaking the law, or preventing them from breaking the law. Critics inside and outside the academy have noted *COPS* for promoting racist and even fascist ideals in the tradition of crime-based reality shows that depict crime as "acts of irrational (and often drug-induced) evil committed by dark-skinned males and promiscuous females. These lawbreakers are a breed of humans different from us who reject many of 'our' cherished social values" (Kooistra, Mahoney, & Westervelt, 1998, p. 142). Furthermore, *COPS* presents each case as a scintillating drama filled with chases and drawn firearms presented as acts of heroism. As punk activist Jello Biafra (1998) notes, *COPS* has conditioned a generation of U.S. Americans (now a second generation) to root for "good guy" police breaking down our neighbors' doors. It is, Biafra observes, a "desensitizing agent to get us to not want to have any human rights anymore." Through its crude construction of lightness versus darkness and hero versus villain presented as a virtual sporting event, *COPS* presents students with a familiar and accessible mediated text with which to practice critical media literacy skills.

COURSE(S):

Introduction to Communication; Public Speaking

OBJECTIVE(S) (NCA, 2015):

- To critically analyze messages
- To apply ethical communication principles and practices
- To utilize communication to embrace difference and influence public discourse

ACTIVITY

This activity can be completed in one 50- or 75-minute period. It requires video clips of *COPS* on DVD or streaming video service and projection technology (e.g., computer and projector). Onscreen subtitles and/or written transcriptions of dialogue are recommended. A worksheet and/or list of discussion prompts are optional and recommended for students with beginning or intermediate understanding of critical media studies.

Before beginning the activity, students should be familiar with 1) the role of mass media and popular culture in crafting our shared social reality; 2) the role of commercial media producers in influencing public awareness of political topics such as race, class, gender, and criminality; 3) the constructed (as opposed to natural or objective) nature of mediated representations of reality (see Hall, 1980); and 4) the possibilities and challenges of audiences accepting or rejecting mediated depictions of reality (see Fiske, 1987; Jenkins, 1992). Students should understand critical media literacy as both a challenge and an opportunity for confronting, denaturalizing, and participating in activism in pursuit of social justice.

Begin the activity by screening the selected clip(s). After screening, students may break into small groups to discuss before reconvening with the large group; depending on the time available and size of the class, the activity can also be completed by classroom discussion without breaking into small groups first, but students should have 5 to 15 minutes to consider questions such as the following:

- What is your initial interpretation of the message of the video clip? Did you initially interpret the clip to be a faithful depiction of reality?
- Who are the characters in the video? Which characters do you understand to be the "good guy(s) and bad guy(s)"? What choices did the producers make to construct heroism and criminality?
- What did the villain do that put him/her in conflict with the police? Did you perceive the act to justify intervention by law enforcement? What information did the video provide that signifies that police intervention was just?
- With whom in the video, if anybody, did you identify? What attractive traits does the character embody, and how does the character perform those traits? Conversely, what undesirable traits are present in characters with whom you do not identify? How does the video emphasize those traits? How are desirable or undesirable traits connected to cultural discourses related to heroism or criminality?
- How does race or ethnicity factor into your understanding of the drama? How does class factor into your understanding of the drama? How does the video construct race and/or class in relation to heroism or criminality?
- How is the drama resolved? Do the characters change in any way? Does the resolution achieve the assumed goal of American criminal justice: crime prevention and rehabilitation? How was justice served, and for whom?

After allotting students time to gather their thoughts and tease out their assumptions alone or in small groups, reconvene the large group and compare ideas. As discussion unfolds, consider students' ideas through a lens of the ways in which the text reifies and/or justifies systems of suffering and marginalization. Can reading the text critically and oppositionally highlight inequities or present opportunities for alternate, more just models of state–citizen relations in regard to law enforcement and breaking the law?

DEBRIEFING

In addition to discussing theories on mediated representation and the constitutive role of commercial mass media, students can continue to explore this topic through assignments such as a short essay, entry in a weekly journal, or informative or persuasive speech. As an example of a more time-intensive follow-up activity, instructors can ask students to conduct research on the real everyday activities of local police. *COPS* does not deign to depict officers making unfruitful or unnecessary stops or engaging in mundane interactions that do not lead to sensational chases and arrests; students could be assigned to interview a local officer to discover how frequently *COPS*-style spectacular crimes and arrests truly occur. Instructors can also arrange for a police officer or criminal justice faculty member to attend class and compare and contrast everyday law enforcement and mediated representations of law enforcement.

REFLEXIVE APPRAISAL

This activity calls on students to participate in a politically charged social debate that may intimidate some students, while prompting incendiary rhetoric from others, which can effectively silence students whose attitudes toward crime and law enforcement differ from the classroom majority. Though this activity is consciously designed to interrogate the attitudes, values, and beliefs undergirding prevailing social discourses on law enforcement and criminality, we should not take for granted a classroom environment in which all students feel equally safe and empowered to discuss their experiences and perceptions.

Instructors should carefully consider the interpersonal dynamics of each unique class and prepare the activity to create space for salient viewpoints that are underrepresented in the classroom discussion. For example, consider a class composed of mostly White, Midwestern students with a relatively smaller number of students of racial or ethnic populations disproportionately targeted by law enforcement. In preparing the activity, instructors can introduce perspectives that challenge mainstream discourses on disproportionately targeted populations and support those perspectives with effective persuasive strategies. Instructors should take special care not to force students to serve as spokespersons for social groups to which they belong; even taking special care to directly or indirectly empower all students to participate and feel empowered will not completely alleviate unequal power dynamics in the classroom. Though the instructor plays a significant role in introducing alternate discourses and dialogically engaging with students to challenge existing beliefs, forcefully confronting and shaming students can have a silencing effect individually and collectively, and can result in a boomerang effect that unwittingly reinforces unproductive and oppressive discourses on the subject.

More diverse classes will include students with both positive and negative experiences interacting with police and law-enforcement agents, which often results in passionate discussion. After participating in this activity in a dialogic, constructive environment, students have expressed feeling empowered by gaining access to a heuristic vocabulary for deconstructing a prominent mediated text that many grew up believing was a faithful depiction of objective reality. Instructors can help promote such an environment by encouraging students to explain their experiences and/or assumptions and to engage with other perspectives, which both promotes dialogue and introspection and further offers avenues for denaturalizing hegemonic discourses on law and criminality.

REFERENCES

Bagdikian, B. H. (2004). *The new media monopoly*. Boston, MA: Beacon Press.

Barthes, R. (1972). *Mythologies*. (A. Lavers, Trans.). New York, NY: Hill and Wang.

Biafra, J. (1998). The new Soviet Union. On *If evolution is outlawed, only outlaws will evolve* [CD]. San Francisco, CA: Alternative Tentacles.

Fiske, J. (1987). *Television culture*. New York, NY: Routledge.

Hall, S. (1980). Encoding/decoding. In S. Hall, D. Hobson, A. Lowe, & P. Willis (Eds.), *Culture, media, language* (pp. 128–138). London, UK: Hutchinson

Jenkins, H. (1992). *Textual poachers: Television fans & participatory culture*. New York, NY: Routledge.

Kooistra, P. G., Mahoney, J. S., & Westervelt, S. D. (1998). The world of crime according to "Cops." In M. Fishman & G. Cavender (Eds.), *Entertaining crime: Television reality programs* (pp. 141–158). New York, NY: Aldine De Gruyter.

NCA. (2015). *Drawing learning outcomes in communication into meaningful practice*. The National Communication Association's Learning Outcomes in Communication Project. Retrieved from https://www.natcom.org/sites/default/files/publications/LOC_2_Drawing_Learning_Outcomes_in_Communication.pdf

Warren, J. T., & Fassett, D. L. (2015). *Communication: A critical/cultural introduction* (2nd ed.). Thousand Oaks, CA: Sage Publications.

ENGAGING IN SOCIAL JUSTICE AND CULTURAL DIVERSITY THROUGH CRITICAL ETHNOGRAPHY

NANCY BRESSLER

RATIONALE

Through this project, students engage in ethnographic research within a community service-learning or nonprofit community organization. Students combine ethnographic fieldwork with community engagement to produce a media presentation that demonstrates how these service-learning organizations enact social change in the local community. Finally, students present and discuss their projects with their classmates through video creation and a class presentation. As they start to inquire and confront ideas, particularly those that appear natural and/ or taken for granted, students take a critical perspective (Warren & Fassett, 2015). Consequently, this assignment provides students the opportunity to take a critical perspective on the inequality that exists within their community. Students utilize ethnographic research to engage in the service-learning organization of their choice to learn about, understand, and appreciate how community organizations impact local citizens. Since ethnography provides for the immersion of a researcher within a culture or organization, it is perfect for community engagement. Students can explore the service-learning organization and its benefits through the point of view of the volunteers and community members with whom the organization members interact. Through critical ethnography, students engage with the organization and its local work in the community.

Critical ethnography provides students the opportunity to critique power differences and take action when observing social problems (Davis, Gallardo, & Lachlan, 2013). The emphasis of critical ethnography is dialogue between the students and members of the culture with which they engage. In particular, "critical service-learning emphasizes communication with the disadvantages about institutions, agencies, and social practices that sustain inequality, providing students with an opportunity to describe, experience, and confront hegemony" (Artz, 2001, p. 242). Consequently, students can situate themselves within the community and be actively engaged in their learning, their community, and the social justice that the service learning advocates for. Active learning activities are those which "involve students in doing things and thinking about what they are doing" (Bonwell & Eison, 1991, p. 1). Previous research has revealed that students who actively engage with course material through classroom activities, rather than lectures, comprehend course content and collaborate with their classmates better (Baepler & Walker, 2014; Bonwell & Eison, 1991; Roehl, Reddy, & Shannon, 2013). Additionally, service-learning research applied to the classroom stresses that social awareness can best be raised through "lived educational methods" (Artz, 2001, p. 239). Through the interaction with service-learning volunteers and those in the community that they help, students can become more aware of the injustice's causes and possible solutions.

COURSE(S):

Introduction to Communication; Communication and Culture; Communication Research

OBJECTIVE(S):

By completing this activity, students should be able to:

- engage in active learning through ethnographic research,
- explain how injustice and/or inequality exists within their community and how the service-learning organizations affect their community,
- employ active learning to embrace cultural diversity and respect diverse perspectives,
- articulate the unique cultural and social perspectives of members of their community,
- identify the similarities and/or differences between the injustices that students' communities face, and
- advocate, through a critical perspective, that oppression is not an individual concern.

ACTIVITY

Students must first decide which service-learning organization they would like to be the focus of their project. Instructors should encourage the students to visit the organization and/or any student resource office on campus to gain more information about their organization before making a final selection.

Once each student has an organization, they will conduct an ethnography of participants within the organization. An ethnography "describes the norms and practices used by people in a particular group or culture" (Merrigan & Huston, 2009, p. 235). Students can complete this part of the project through critical ethnography, which studies how power and control are enacted and sustained. By completing a critical ethnography, students can "see the possibility of [their] participation resulting in changes to social problems" (Davis, Gallardo, & Lachlan, 2013, p. 327). A critical ethnography can demonstrate how community members can take action to challenge the status quo. Students could use this type of critical ethnography to critique a social or community issue and then question to what extent the service-learning organization is able to enact social change. As Thomas (1993) argues, critical ethnography is more than reporting on a subject and instead strives to "empower the subject's voice and use that knowledge for change" (p. 3). Through the interaction with the service-learning volunteers and those they work with in the community, students can enhance their awareness because of critical ethnography.

After students have selected their choice of ethnography, they also need to conduct some participant observations and/or informal interviews with service-learning volunteers and members of the community. My recommendation would be at least two separate observations and two interviews to maximize the information gathered. In particular, instructors should emphasize that student's work with the service-learning organizations; the more time that students spend in critical service-learning opportunities, the more likely it is they will understand how the organization strives to overcome the conditions of inequality (Artz, 2001).

Finally, students create their final video presentation to share with their classmates and discuss what they have learned from the experience. Using video creation software, students creatively showcase the service-learning organization's efforts and demonstrate how these organizations benefit the community. Videos should be 10 to 12 minutes long and posted on the class YouTube site. Students then review each other's videos to understand and appreciate the community engagement of each service-learning organization. Rather than listen to authoritative discourse from the instructor, students engage in dialogue about what they have learned from the project. Dialogic engagement in the classroom encourages students to present their own interpretations without evaluation from the teacher (Kaufmann, 2010). Consequently, students' discussions about their experiences provide students both a voice through dialogue and awareness of community concerns.

DEBRIEFING

During the final two weeks of classes, students prepare a short 4-to-6-minute informative presentation on their experience with the project. During the presentation (and in preparation for the final presentation), students should be able to answer the following questions:

1. What have you learned as a result of this experience?
2. What do you feel you accomplished and/or how do you feel you made an impact on the community with this project?
3. How have the organization, this project, and/or you become an advocate for social change in the community or on a broader level?

REFLEXIVE APPRAISAL

Students appreciate using ethnographic research to learn more about the service-learning organization and its impact on their community. As opposed to listening to a lecture, students are actively engaged in a class project that highlights how their community can be impacted by the organization they select. Through the use of a media creation rather than writing a paper about the organization, students are also more involved in the project. To maximize the benefits of this project, instructors should stress that students not only spend time with the volunteers, but truly engage with the members of the community who face inequality.

Giroux (2009) encouraged instructors to take on the challenge of disallowing the ideology that social problems are individual problems and naturalistic in design. Because of the dialogue about their projects, students often observe similarities and differences among their experiences and how ideology and power are larger entities than just within one community concern. Critical ethnography provides a method for instructors to emphasize not only awareness for oppression, but also advocacy for the social issue. Inequality is sustained when people remain unaware of the problem and the causes of an issue. Through service-learning activities, particularly critical ethnography, students can challenge hegemonic concerns within their community because of their experiences with members of the community who face these injustices.

SUGGESTED READINGS

Conquergood, D. (1991). Rethinking ethnography: Towards a critical cultural politics. *Communication Monographs*, 58(2), 179–194.

Davis, C. S., Gallardo, H. P., & Lachlan, K. A. (2013). *Straight talk about communication research methods* (2nd ed.). Dubuque, IA: Kendall-Hunt.

Madison, D. S. (2011). *Critical ethnography: Method, ethics, and performance.* Thousand Oaks, CA: Sage Publications.

Merrigan, G., & Huston, C. (2009). *Communication research methods* (2nd ed.). New York, NY: Oxford University Press.

Murchison, J. (2009). *Ethnography essentials: Designing, conducting, and presenting your research.* San Francisco, CA: John Wiley & Sons.

Townsend, R. M. (2013). Engaging "others" in civic engagement through ethnography of communication. *Journal of Applied Communication Research, 41*(2), 202–208.

Wolcott, H. F. (2008). *Ethnography: A way of seeing.* Lanham, MD: Rowman & Littlefield Publishers Inc.

REFERENCES

Artz, L. (2001). Critical ethnography for communication studies: Dialogue and social justice in service-learning. *Southern Communication Journal, 66*(3), 239–250. doi: 10.1080/10417940109373202

Baepler, P., & Walker, J. D. (2014). Active learning classrooms and educational alliances: Changing relationships to improve learning. *New Directions for Teaching & Learning, 2014*(137), 27–40. doi: 10.1002/tl.20083

Bonwell, C. C., & Eison, J. A. (1991). *Active learning: Creating excitement in the classroom.* Washington, DC: School of Education and Human Development, George Washington University.

Davis, C. S., Gallardo, H. P., & Lachlan, K. A. (2013). *Straight talk about communication research methods* (2nd ed.). Dubuque, IA: Kendall-Hunt.

Giroux, H. A. (2009). Cultural studies, critical pedagogy, and the politics of higher education. In R. Hammer & D. Kellner (Eds.), *Media/cultural studies: Critical approaches* (pp. 88–106). New York, NY: Peter Lang.

Kaufmann, J. J. (2010). The practice of dialogue in critical pedagogy. *Adult Education Quarterly, 60*(5), 456–476.

Merrigan, G., & Huston, C. (2009). *Communication research methods* (2nd ed.). New York, NY: Oxford University Press.

Roehl, A., Reddy, S. L., & Shannon, G. J. (2013). The flipped classroom: An opportunity to engage millennial students through active learning strategies. *Journal of Family & Consumer Sciences, 105*(2), 44–49.

Thomas, J. (1993). *Doing critical ethnography.* Newbury Park, CA: Sage Publications.

Warren, J. T., & Fassett, D. L. (2015). *Communication: A critical/cultural introduction.* Thousand Oaks, CA: Sage Publications.

POSTING PERCEPTIONS: ACKNOWLEDGING PATTERNS AND POTENTIAL SUBCONSCIOUS BIASES

SARAH E. RIFORGIATE

RATIONALE

We cannot change what we have experienced or learned in the past, but we *can* be thoughtful moving forward, reflecting on belief systems to make choices about future communication (Allen, 2014). Yet, frequently students come to the classroom with expectations that are largely unquestioned, shaping their worldview and resulting communication (Allen, 2005). When we don't recognize and acknowledge our belief systems, we do something that Allen (2014) calls "thinking under the influence"; in other words, we communicate using assumptions and automatic responses rather than mindfully engaging in communication in a thoughtful and informed manner. Mindful communication is not about erasing differences, but about recognizing and celebrating differences to treat individuals with compassion and dignity (Allen, 2011). To do so, we can use critical communication pedagogy which "is about engaging the classroom as a site of social influence. ... It is about respecting teachers and students and the possible actions they can take, however small, to effect material change to the people and the world around them" (Fassett & Warren, 2007, p. 6).

Conversations about existing belief systems can be uncomfortable, making students feel guilty, chastised, and even singled out. However, there are productive ways to engage students to help them recognize underlying value systems and biases, and to discuss why these systems exist (Practicing a pedagogy that engages diversity, 2012). Allowing students to generate activity material in a non-threatening way increases the likelihood they will take part in self-reflection and discussion (hooks, 1994). Further, incorporating active learning strategies enhances student engagement, deepens information processing and memory (Sousa, 2011), and improves learning across a diverse group of students (Milem, 2001).

COURSE(S):

Introduction to Communication; Public Speaking; Interpersonal Communication

OBJECTIVE(S):

- In line with NCA's learning outcomes in communication (NCA, 2015), analyzing and challenging dominant representations of success in society creates an opportunity for students to
- critically analyze messages,
- apply ethical communication principles and practices,
- utilize communication to embrace difference, and
- influence public discourses.

REQUIRED MATERIALS:

Post-it notes, white or chalk board, dry erase pens or chalk

ACTIVITY

Although this activity is relatively simple to enact in class, it is a powerful tool that allows students to think about their own and others' perceptions, including why these perceptions exist and continue. To prepare for this activity, bring a Post-it note for each student; I generally pass a pad of Post-it notes around the class and ask everyone to take one. You will also need a white or chalk board available, and something to write on it with (i.e., dry erase marker or chalk). If you have a large lecture class, you could adapt this activity using a clicker system, PowerPoint, and projector screen.

Depending on the focus of your class, begin the class by asking students to think of a "Great Speaker" or to think of a "Great Leader" and to write that person's name down on the Post-it note (or, for a large lecture class, students can write in their class notes). Encourage students to put down the first person that comes to mind and only give them a minute to write the name down. Students often ask if the person has to be someone famous; explain this is not necessary, it can be anyone they consider a great speaker or leader.

Once everyone has finished writing, draw a giant intersecting vertical and horizontal line on the board, labeling the anchors on the vertical line "Male" and "Female" and the anchors on the horizontal line "White" or "Person of Color." Also make sure to talk with students about the diversity within the "Person of Color" category and acknowledge that this is a rudimentary grouping to allow for a simple visual representation.

Then ask students to place their Post-it note in one of the four quadrants that describes the demographic characteristics of the great speaker or leader they wrote down (White male, White female, person of color male, or person of color female). If you are using a clicker system, create these four categories as numbered options that display as a graph or pie chart and have the students click on the description where their leader fits.

Ask students to form pairs or small groups and give them about five minutes to talk about the following discussion prompts:

- What are the trends in perceptions of great speakers and leaders in this activity?
- In what ways are these trends accurate and biased?
- What are possible explanations for these trends?
- How do these trends influence the ways we associate a great speaker or leader with particular characteristics?
- In what ways are the perceptions represented constructive and harmful?

Once students have time to discuss, open up the conversation to the full class and have students share answers. Be sure to ask follow-up questions such as, "Why do you think that is the case?" or inviting, "Tell me more about that idea."

DEBRIEFING

Every time I have led this activity, overwhelmingly the White male category has the greatest representation. Depending on the class size, often no one includes a great speaker or leader in the person of color female category. This provides an important visual representation that leads to fruitful discussion. Ultimately, the goal is to have students recognize biases that exist and consider how these biases influence perceptions of other speakers or leaders. It is important to point out that more White males are in speaker and leadership positions, which explains part of the trend. However, there are speakers and leaders in all of the quadrants. By immediately thinking of great speakers and leaders as White males, we miss out on opportunities to embrace diverse leadership and limit possibilities for those who do not fall in this dominant category. Conclude the conversation by asking students to give examples of great speakers and leaders who are not well-represented in some of the quadrants.

REFLEXIVE APPRAISAL

As a White female, I recognize that my demographic position allows me to talk about inequities in representation in particular ways (not from the dominant White male group, but also not in the people of color groups). In some ways this is a liminal space where I am in-between (Fassett & Warren, 2007), and I make that explicit in our class discussions. It is frustrating that one category tends to be saturated while the others are not—that *my* category has very few examples generated by the class. However, unless students can see and recognize these patterns, they will likely not question their perceptions. I make sure to explain that there are plenty of examples in all four quadrants; my goal is not to discredit any of the speakers or leaders, but to make space for the idea that speakers and leaders come from all demographic characteristics, using an additive framework (where more great speakers/leaders are always needed). More representation in one quadrant does not devalue the contribution of those in another quadrant; it makes space to recognize that there are important contributions across demographic characteristics.

Discussion can be extended by asking, "How might we change the way we think about speakers and leaders through communication?" and "How might we overcome assumptions based on nonverbal cues?" In addition, students can re-collect their Post-it notes and organize them a second time by changing the labels. For example, anchor descriptions could be changed to tap into gender (Masculine/Feminine), sexuality (Attraction to Opposite Sex/Same Sex), power (Legitimate Power/Referent Power), age (Under 30/Over 30) or any range of demographic characteristics.

Engaged learning practices help students think about concepts in new ways and apply learning to future encounters. Using this activity and leading a healthy discussion allows students to recognize perceptions about diversity and biases pertaining to speakers and leaders, and to think mindfully about their assumptions and communication moving forward. As Postman and Weingartner (1969) explain, "the ability to learn can be seen as the ability to relinquish inappropriate perceptions and develop new – and more workable – ones" (p. 90). Through participating in this activity, students are able to increase awareness, allowing for meaningful learning to occur.

REFERENCES

Allen, B. J. (2005). Social constructionism. In S. May & D. Mumby (Eds.), *Engaging organizational communication theory and research: Multiple perspectives* (pp. 35–53). Thousand Oaks, CA: Sage Publications.

Allen, B. J. (2011). *Difference matters: Communicating social identity* (2nd ed.). Long Grove, IL: Waveland Press.

Allen, B. J. (2014). *Teaching difference matters.* Holland, MI: National Communication Association Institute for Faculty Development.

Fassett, D. L., & Warren, J. T. (2007). *Critical communication pedagogy.* Thousand Oaks, CA: Sage Publications.

hooks, b. (1994). *Teaching to transgress: Education as the practice of freedom.* New York, NY: Routledge.

Lee, L., Poch, R., Shaw, M., & Williams, R. (2012). Practicing a pedagogy that engages diversity. *ASHE Higher Education Report, 38*(2), 83–101.

Milem, J. F. (2001). *Increasing diversity benefits: How campus climate and teaching methods affect student outcomes.* Retrieved from http://files.eric.ed.gov/fulltext/ED456202.pdf.

NCA. (2015). *Drawing learning outcomes in communication into meaningful practice.* The National Communication Association's Learning Outcomes in Communication Project. Retrieved from https://www.natcom.org/sites/default/files/publications/LOC_2_Drawing_Learning_Outcomes_in_Communication.pdf

Postman, N., & Weingartner, C. (1969). *Teaching as a subversive activity*. New York, NY: Dell Publishing Co., Inc.

Sousa, D. A. (2011). *How the brain learns* (4th ed.). Thousand Oaks, CA: Corwin Press.

ACTIVITY 16

BE THE CHANGE: CARDBOARD CONFESSIONALS

NICHOLAS T. TATUM AND T. KODY FREY

RATIONALE

This course-culminating, critically oriented activity is designed to help students reflect on course concepts and experiences, and how they relate to critiquing and changing power relations in society. Rather than "indoctrinate students to accept dominant ideologies" (Allen, 2011, p. 104), this activity seeks to help students identify their role in enacting social change through radical reflexivity (Fassett & Warren, 2007)—considering the way communication, community, and the common good interact to promote personal, professional, and societal benefits (Simonds, Hunt, & Simonds, 2013). Therefore, this activity should be used as a concluding activity for the course, in which students think about how to best utilize their freshly honed communication skills. By the end of the activity, students should be able to recognize the particular social justice issues that matter to them, critically reflect on the ways in which they can use communication concepts to undermine oppressive and unjust ideologies, and identify specific steps for taking action.

COURSE(S):

Introduction to Communication

OBJECTIVE(S):

- Empower individuals to promote human rights, human dignity, and human freedom.
- Identify the social justice challenges facing communities and the role of communication in resolving those challenges.
- Utilize communication to respond to social justice issues at the local level.
- Select creative and appropriate modalities and technologies to accomplish communicative goals.
- Make progress towards public speaking proficiency.

MATERIALS:

Mid-sized pieces of cardboard, permanent markers, and adhesive

ACTIVITY

1. **Introduction (5 min):** To introduce the assignment and capture the students' attention, play the following video that utilizes cardboard confessionals to communicate about social justice issues.
   - https://www.youtube.com/watch?v=2G5ejhD9UpY
2. **Issue Selection (7 min):** Give each student a piece of cardboard, a permanent marker, and a piece of adhesive. Instruct students to write a word, phrase, or sentence describing a social justice issue they find personally captivating. Upon completion, have students post these "cardboard confessionals" to the walls of the classroom using the adhesive provided.
   - Examples: health disparities, human trafficking, homelessness
3. **Issue Organization (10 min):** As an instructor, lead the class in physically organizing the posted issues into categories. There is no "right" way to organize the selected topics—the organization process simply serves as an opportunity to think more critically about social justice.
   - Example categories: health, wealth, race, human rights, unequal treatment

4. **Discussion (20 min):** Lead the class in a discussion using the following questions:
    - In what areas of the world are these social justice concerns present?
    - Can all social justice issues be combatted in the same way?
    - What is currently being done to combat these issues?
    - Are you doing anything to make a difference regarding your chosen issue?

5. **Introduction of Assignment (7 min):** At the completion of the discussion, introduce the "Be the Change: Cardboard Confessionals" speech. As a way to wrap up the semester, each student will construct and deliver a four-to-five-minute speech that outlines ways he or she can make a difference in combatting a selected social justice issue. **Allow students approximately two weeks to complete this assignment.** Speeches should
    - be contextualized to an explicit location (city, county, or region),
    - provide current information regarding the realities of their chosen issue,
    - elaborate on two or three course-specific concepts or skills that can be used to make a difference regarding their chosen issue, and
    - utilize a visual aid with compelling information and design.

6. **Speech Delivery (1–2 class periods)**

DEBRIEFING

After each student has delivered their speech, lead the class in a discussion using several of the following questions:

- What concepts or skills presented in this course were shown to be effective tools for combatting social justice?
- Using what you know about communication, what are some actual steps that you can take to produce long-lasting social change?
- Should all social justice issues be combatted in the same way? Why or why not? **Note:** All social justice issues are unique and have varying causes, perpetuations, and inequalities. Because of this, each issue needs to be engaged uniquely.

- If you can't physically travel to the location where a social justice issue is occurring, what steps can be taken to still make a difference?
- How does what you learned in this course relate to your position as a citizen in a democratic society?
- What did you gain as a result of completing this activity?

REFLEXIVE APPRAISAL

Essentially, this activity is about allowing instructors to create a dialogue with students surrounding contradictions of power, privilege, and freedom in their communities. Students will critically reflect on issues that are personally important to them, regardless of classmate or teacher opinion, and identify the appropriate steps for breaking down barriers through the communication concepts they learned over the semester. When conducting this activity, it is important for instructors to recognize that students will inherently be interested in a variety of different topics. Instructors must have the critical knowledge to connect various student interests to larger, more abstract patterns of social justice. Without this recognition, students are at risk of pursuing interests that do not fit within the scope of asymmetrical privilege, failing to understand the dominant ideologies that marginalize members of society, or looking negatively upon the differences between various racial, ethnic, or sociocultural identities.

Additionally, instructors must take caution to guide students toward narrow notions of change that could be pursued following the conclusion of the course. Finally, it is paramount that instructors address the communicative ethics that surround this assignment. Without examples of the ways in which multiple perspectives influence the issues being addressed, students might not realize how ethical standards may be interpreted differently among various constituents. As an activity designed for the basic communication course, this dialogic experience will allow instructors to affirm their students' sense of self-worth through the identification and realization of newly developed skills that can be realistically implemented. Ultimately, this activity represents a great opportunity to introduce students to higher-order communication concepts and ideas while developing public-speaking proficiencies in a socially just and relevant manner.

REFERENCES

Allen, B. J. (2011). Critical communication pedagogy as a framework for teaching difference and organizing. In D. K. Mumby (Ed.), *Reframing difference in organizational communication studies: Research, pedagogy, and practice* (pp. 103–125). Thousand Oaks, CA: Sage Publications.

Fassett, D., & Warren, J. (2007). *Critical communication pedagogy.* Thousand Oaks, CA: Sage Publications.

Simonds, C. J., Hunt, S. K., & Simonds, B. K. (2013). *Communication as critical inquiry* (5th ed. for Illinois State University). Boston, MA: Pearson Custom Publishing.

REFERENCES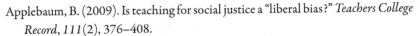

Applebaum, B. (2009). Is teaching for social justice a "liberal bias?" *Teachers College Record, 111*(2), 376–408.

Barros, S. R. (2011). Terms of engagement: Reframing Freirean-based assessment in institutional education. *Rangsit Journal of Arts and Sciences, 1*(1), 79–87.

Bell, L. A. (2007). Theoretical foundations for social justice education. In M. Adams, L. A. Bell, & P. Griffin (Eds.), *Teaching for diversity and social justice* (2nd ed.; pp. 1–14). New York, NY: Routledge.

Blair, T. (2007). The syllabus as a communication document: Constructing and presenting a syllabus. *Communication Education, 56,* 54–71. doi: 10.1080/03634520601011575

Burroughs, N. (2007). A reinvestigation of the relationship of teacher nonverbal immediacy and student compliance-resistance with learning. *Communication Education, 56*(4), 453–475. doi: 10.1080/03634520701530896

Butler, J. (1990). *Gender trouble: Feminism and the subversion of identity.* New York, NY: Routledge.

Carr, D. L., Davies, T. L., & Lavin, A. M. (2010). The impact of instructor attire on college student satisfaction. *College Student Journal, 44*(1), 101–111.

Clump, M. A., Bauer, H., & Whiteleather, A. (2003). To attend or not to attend: Is that a good question? *Journal of Instructional Psychology, 30*(3), 220–224.

Collins, P. H. (2000). *Black feminist thought: Knowledge, consciousness, and the politics of empowerment* (rev. ed.). New York, NY: Routledge.

Conquergood, D. (2002). Performance studies: Interventions and radical research. *TDR: The Drama Review, 46*(2), 145–156.

Cooper, C., & Odell, L. (1971). *Evaluating writing: Describing, measuring, judging.* Urbana, IL: National Council of Teachers of English.

Craig, R. T. (1999). Communication theory as a field. *Communication Theory, 9,* 119–161. doi: 10.1111/j.1468-2885.1999.tb00355.x

Credé, M., Roch, S. G., & Kieszczynka, U. M. (2010). Class attendance in college: A meta-analytic review of the relationship of class attendance with grades and student characteristics. *Review of Educational Research, 80*(2), 272–295. doi: 10.3102/0034654310362998

Crenshaw, K. (1991). Mapping the margins: Intersectionality, identity politics, and violence against women of color. *Stanford Law Review, 43*(6), 1241–1279.

Danielewicz, J., & Elbow, P. (2009). A unilateral grading contract to improve learning and teaching. *College Composition and Communication, 61*(2), 244–268.

Dannels, D. (2014). *Eight essential questions teachers ask: A guidebook for communicating with students.* New York, NY: Oxford University Press.

Darder, A. (1991). *Culture and power in the classroom: A critical foundation for bicultural education.* Westport, CT: Bergin & Garvey.

Delpit, L. (1988). The silenced dialogue: Power and pedagogy in educating other people's children. *Harvard Educational Review, 58*(3), 280–299.

DeTurk, S. (2006). The power of dialogue: Consequences of intergroup dialogue and their implications for agency and alliance building. *Communication Quarterly, 54*(1), 33–51. doi: 10.1080/01463370500270355

DeTurk, S. (2011). Allies in action: The communicative experiences of people who challenge social injustice on behalf of others. *Communication Quarterly, 59*(5), 569–590. doi: 10.1080/01463373.2011.614209

Dewey, J. (1916). *Democracy and education: An introduction to the philosophy of education.* New York, NY: The Free Press.

DiAngelo, R. (2011). White fragility. *International Journal of Critical Pedagogy, 3*(3), 54–70.

Fassett, D. L., & Rudick, C. K. (2016). Critical communication pedagogy. In P. L. Witt (Ed.), *Handbooks of communication science: Communication and learning* (vol. 16, pp. 573–598). Berlin, Germany: DeGruyter Mouton.

Fassett, D. L., & Warren, J. T. (2007). *Critical communication pedagogy.* Thousand Oaks, CA: Sage Publications.

Freire, P. (1994). *Pedagogy of hope.* New York, NY: Continuum International.

Freire, P. (2000). *Pedagogy of the oppressed.* New York, NY: Continuum International.

Frey, L. R., & Palmer, D. L. (Eds.). (2014). *Teaching communication activism: Communication education for social justice.* New York, NY: Hampton Press.

Frey, L. R., Pearce, W. B., Pollock, M. A., Artz, L., & Murphy, B. A. O. (1996). Looking for justice in all the wrong places: On a communicative approach to social justice. *Communication Studies, 47*(1-2), 110–127.

Gatto, J. T. (2006). *Dumbing us down: The hidden curriculum of compulsory schooling.* Gabriola Island, British Columbia: New Society Publishers.

Gehrke, P. P., & Keith, W. M. (Eds.) (2015). *A century of communication studies: The unfinished conversation.* New York, NY: Routledge.

Giroux, H. A., & Penna, A. (1983). Social education in the classroom: The dynamics of the hidden curriculum. In H. Giroux & D. Purpel (Eds.), *Hidden curriculum and moral education: Deception or discovery?* (pp. 100–121). Berkeley, CA: McCutchan Publishing.

Goffman, E. (1959). *The presentation of self in everyday life.* New York, NY: Doubleday.

Golsan, K. B., & Rudick, C. K. (2015). Caught in the rhetoric: How students with disabilities are framed by DSS offices in U.S. higher education. In A. Atay & M. Ashlock (Eds.), *The discourse of disability in communication education: Narrative-based research for social change.* New York, NY: Peter Lang.

Gorham, J., & Cohen, S. H. (1999). Fashion in the classroom III: Effects of instructor attire and immediacy in natural classroom interactions. *Communication Quarterly, 47*(3), 281–299. doi: 10.1080/01463379909385560

Gorham, J., Morris, T. L., & Cohen, S. H. (1997). Fashion in the classroom II: Instructor immediacy and attire. *Communication Research Reports, 14*(1), 11–23. doi: 10.1080/08824099709388641

Greene, M. (2000). *Releasing the imagination: Essays on education, the arts, and social change.* San Francisco, CA: Jossey-Bass.

Gullicks, K., Pearson, J., Child, J., & Schwab, C. (2005). Diversity and power in public speaking textbooks. *Communication Quarterly, 53,* 247–258. doi:10.1080/01463370500089870

Gump, S. E. (2005). The cost of cutting class: Attendance as a predictor of student success. *College Teacher, 53,* 21–26. doi: 10.3200/CTCH.53.1.21-26

Hao, R. N. (2011). Rethinking critical pedagogy: Implications on silence and silent bodies. *Text and Performance Quarterly, 31,* 267–284. doi:10.1080/10462937.2011.573185

Hardiman, R., & Jackson, B., & Griffin, P. (2007). Conceptual foundation for social justice education. In M. Adams, L. A. Bell, & P. Griffin, *Teaching for diversity and social justice* (2nd ed.; pp. 35–66). New York, NY: Routledge.

Hendrix, K. G., & Wilson, C. (2014). Virtual invisibility: Race and communication education. *Communication Education*, 63(4), 405–428. doi:10.1080/036 34523.2014.934852

Hendrix, K., Jackson, R. L., & Warren, J. R. (2003). Shifting academic landscapes: Exploring co-identities, identity negotiation, and critical progressive pedagogy. *Communication Education*, 52, 177–190. doi:10.1080/0363452032000156 181

Hendrix, K., Mazer, J. P., & Hess, J. A. (2016). Editor's introduction: Interrogating the darkness. *Communication Education*, 65(1), 105–107. doi: 10.1080/03634523.2015.1110247

hooks, b. (1994). *Teaching to transgress: Education as the practice of freedom*. New York, NY: Routledge.

Horton, M., & Freire, P. (1990). *We make the road while walking: Conversations on education and social change*. Philadelphia, PA: Temple University.

Hytten, K., & Warren, J. T. (2003). Engaging whiteness: How racial power gets reified in education. *International Journal of Qualitative Studies in Education*, 16, 65–89. doi:10.1080/0951839032000033509a

Johnston, B. (2004). Summative assessment of portfolios: An examination of different approaches to agreement over outcomes. *Studies in Higher Education*, 29, 395–412. doi: 10.1080/03075070410001682646

Kahl, D. H., Jr. (2010). Connecting autoethnography with service learning: A critical communication pedagogical approach. *Communication Teacher*, 24, 221–228. doi:10.1080/17404622.2010.513036

Kahl, D. H., Jr. (2011). Autoethnography as pragmatic scholarship: Moving critical communication pedagogy from ideology to praxis. *International Journal of Communication*, 5, 1927–1946.

Kahl, D. H., Jr. (2013). Critical communication pedagogy and assessment: Reconciling two seemingly incongruous ideas. *International Journal of Communication*, 7, 2610–2630.

Kanpol, B. (1999). *Critical pedagogy: An introduction* (2nd ed.). Westport, CT: Bergin & Garvey.

Knight, M. (2011). The power of assessment. *Business Communication Quarterly*, 74(3), 245–246. doi:10.1177/1080569911420251

Kohn, A. (2011). The case against grades. *Educational Leadership*, 69(3), 28–33.

Lynch, B. K. (2001). Rethinking assessment from a critical perspective. *Language & Testing, 18*, 351–372. doi: 10.1177/026553220101800403

Madison, D. S. (2006). The dialogic performative in critical ethnography. *Text and Performance Quarterly, 26*(4), 320-324. doi: 10.1080/10462930600828675

Madison, D. S. (2011). The labor of reflexivity. *Critical Studies <=> Cultural Methodologies, 11*(2), 129–138. doi: 10.1177/1532708611401331

Marranca, B. (1985). Acts of criticism. *Performing Arts Journal, 9*(1), 9–11.

Matveeva, N. (2007). The intercultural component in textbooks for teaching a service technical writing course. *Journal of Technical Writing and Communication, 37*(2), 151–166.

McGarrity, M. (2010). Communication textbooks: From the publisher to the desk. In D. L. Fassett & J. T. Warren (Eds.), *The SAGE handbook of communication and instruction* (pp. 107–128). Thousand Oaks, CA: Sage Publications.

McKenzie, M. (2014). *Black girl dangerous: On race, queerness, class and gender.* Oakland, CA: BGD Press.

McLaren, P. (2002). *Life in schools: An introduction to critical pedagogy in the foundations of education.* New York, NY: Allyn & Bacon.

Morris, T. L., Gorham, J., Cohen, S. H., & Huffman, D. (1996). Fashion in the classroom: Effects of attire on student perceptions of instructors in college classes. *Communication Education, 45*, 135–148.

Myerson, M., Crawley, S. L., Anstey, E. H., & Okopny, C. (2007). Who's zoomin' who? A feminist, queer content analysis of "interdisciplinary" human sexuality textbooks. *Hypatia, 22*(1), 92–113.

NCA. (2015). *Drawing learning outcomes in communication into meaningful practice.* The National Communication Association's Learning Outcomes in Communication Project. Retrieved from https://www.natcom.org/sites/default/files/publications/LOC_2_Drawing_Learning_Outcomes_in_Communication.pdf

Patton, T. O. (1999). Ethnicity and gender: An examination of its impact on instructor credibility in the university classroom. *The Howard Journal of Communications, 10*(2), 123–144. doi: 10.1080/106461799246852

Patton, T. O. (2004). In the guise of civility: The complicitous maintenance of inferential forms of sexism and racism in higher education. *Women's Studies in Communication, 27*, 60–87. doi: 10.1080/07491409.2004.10162466

Pierce, C. (1995). Stress analogs of racism and sexism: Terrorism, torture, and disaster. In C. Willie, P. Rieker, B. Kramer, & B. Brown (Eds.), *Mental health, racism, and sexism* (pp. 277–293). Pittsburgh, PA: University of Pittsburgh Press.

Pyles, L. (2014). *Progressive community organizing: Reflective practice in a globalizing world* (2nd ed.). New York, NY: Routledge.

Roach, K. D. (1997). Effects of graduate teaching assistant attire on student learning, misbehaviors, and ratings of instruction. *Communication Quarterly, 45*(3), 125–141. doi: 10.1080/01463379709370056

Robson, D. (2001). Women and minorities in economics textbooks: Are they being adequately represented? *The Journal of Economic Education, 32*(2), 186–191.

Rodriguez, P. H. (2015, June 8). Caitlyn Jenner, social media and violent "solidarity": Why calling out abusive material by sharing it is harmful. *Blackgirldangerous*. Retrieved from http://www.blackgirldangerous.org/2015/06/caitlyn-jenner-social-media-and-violent-solidarity-calling-out-abusive-material-sharing-it/.

Rudick, C. K., & Golsan, K. B. (2014). Revisiting the relational communication perspective: Drawing upon relational dialectics theory to map an expanded research agenda for communication and instruction scholarship. *Western Journal of Communication, 78*, 255–273. doi:10.1080/10570314.2014.905796

Russ, T. L., Simonds, C. J., & Hunt, S. K. (2002). Coming out in the classroom ... An occupational hazard? The influence of sexual orientation on teacher credibility and perceived student learning. *Communication Education, 51*, 311–324. doi: 10.1080/03634520216516

Schaull, R. (2006). Foreword. In P. Freire (Ed.), *Pedagogy of the oppressed* (pp. 29–35). New York, NY: Continuum International.

Shor, I. (2009). Critical pedagogy is too big to fail. *Journal of Basic Writing, 28*(2), 6–27.

Simpson, J. L. (2008). The color-blind double bind: Whiteness and the (im) possibility of dialogue. *Communication Theory, 18*, 139–159. doi: 10.1111/j.1468-2885.2007.00317.x

Spencer, L. G., & Capuzza, J. C. (2016). Centering gender identity and transgender lives in instructional communication. *Communication Education, 65*, 113–117. doi: 10.1080/03634523.2015.1096949

Sprague, J. (1992). Expanding the research agenda for instructional communication: Raising some unasked questions. *Communication Education*, *41*, 1–25. doi:10.1080/03634529209378867

Sprague, J. (1993). Retrieving the research agenda for communication education: Asking the pedagogical questions that are "embarrassments to theory." *Communication Education*, *42*, 106–122. doi:10.1080/03634529309378919

Sprague, J. (1994). Ontology, politics, and instructional communication research: Why we can't just "agree to disagree" about power. *Communication Education*, *43*, 273–290. doi:10.1080/03634529409378986

Sprague, J. (2002). Communication education: The spiral continues. *Communication Education*, *51*, 337–354. doi:10.1080/03634520216532

Staton, A. Q. (1989). The interface of communication and instruction: Conceptual considerations and programmatic manifestations. *Communication Education*, *38*, 364–371. doi: 10.1080/03634528909378777

Sue, D. W. (2010). *Microaggressions in everyday life: Race, gender, and sexual orientation*. Hoboken, NJ: John Wiley & Sons.

Sulé, V. T. (2011). Restructuring the master's tools: Black female and Latina faculty navigating and contributing in classrooms through oppositional positions. *Equity & Excellence in Education*, *44*, 169–187. doi: 10.1080/10665684.2011.559415

Thompson, A. (2003). Tiffany, friend of people of color: White investments in antiracism. *Qualitative Studies in Education*, *16*(1), 7–29. doi: 10.1080/0951839032000033509

Verderber, R. F. (1991). The introductory communication course: The public speaking approach. *Basic Communication Course Annual*, *3*, 3–15.

Warren, J. T. (2009). Critical communication pedagogy. In S. Littlejohn & K. Foss (Eds.), *Encyclopedia of communication theory* (pp. 213–216). Thousand Oaks, CA: Sage Publications.

Warren, J. T. (2011). Social justice and critical/performative/communicative pedagogy: A storied account of research, teaching, love, identity, desire and loss. *International Review of Qualitative Research*, *4*, 21–34. doi:10.1177/1532708611401332

Warren, J. T., & Fassett, D. L. (2014). *Communication: A critical/cultural introduction* (2nd ed.). Thousand Oaks, CA: Sage Publications.

Warren, J. T., & Hytten, K. (2004). The faces of whiteness: Pitfalls and the critical democrat. *Communication Education*, 53, 321–340. doi:10.1080/036345203200030593

Yosso, T. J. (2005). Whose culture has capital? A critical race theory discussion of community cultural wealth. *Race Ethnicity and Education*, 8, 69–91. doi:10.1080/1361332052000341006

Zinn, H. (2001). *A people's history of the United States: 1492–present*. New York, NY: Perennial Books.

SUGGESTED READINGS

TEACHING CRITICAL INQUIRY AND SOCIALLY JUST COMMUNICATION

Kaomea, J. (2003). Reading erasures and making the familiar strange: Defamiliar-
izing methods for research in formerly colonized and historically oppressed
communities. *Educational Researcher*, 32(2), 14–25.

Kaomea, J. (2005). Indigenous studies in the elementary curriculum: A cautionary
Hawaiian example. *Anthropology and Education Quarterly*, 36(1), 24–42.

EXPLORING HOW COMMUNICATION IS CENTRAL TO SOCIAL JUSTICE ACTIVISM

Nagler, M. N. (2014). *The nonviolence handbook: A guide for practical action.* San
Francisco, CA: Berrett-Koehler Publishers.

Sandlin, J. A., Schultz, B. D., & Burdick, J. (2010). *Handbook of public pedagogy:
Education and learning beyond schooling.* New York, NY: Taylor & Francis.

Sharp, G. (1973). *The politics of nonviolent action: Part two, the methods of nonviolent action.* New York, NY: Porter Sargent Publishers.

ENGAGING SOCIAL JUSTICE EMPATHY THROUGH INTERPERSONAL COMMUNICATION

Pedersen, P. (2008). A response to "social privilege, social justice, and group
counseling: An inquiry": Inclusive cultural empathy and the search for
social justice. *The Journal for Specialists in Group Work*, 33(4), 370–376. doi:
10.1080/01933920802424431

Tinkler, B., Hannah, C. L., Tinkler, A., & Miller, E. (2015). The impact of a social
justice service-learning field experience in a social foundations course. *Critical
Questions in Education*, 6(1), 16–29.

Tyler, A. (2013). Understanding human security: Traversing the intersection
between social justice and international conflict management. In H. Kim
(Ed.), *A just world: Multi-disciplinary perspectives on social justice* (pp. 69–85).
Newcastle upon Tyne, UK: Cambridge Scholars Publishing.

ENGAGING IN SOCIAL JUSTICE AND CULTURAL DIVERSITY THROUGH CRITICAL ETHNOGRAPHY

Jensen, J. M., & Worth, B. (2014). Valuable knowledge: Students as consumers of critical thinking in the community college classroom. *Journal of General Education*, 63(4), 287–308.

Kinloch, V., Nemeth, E., & Patterson, A. (2015). Reframing service-learning as learning and participation with urban youth. *Theory into Practice*, 54(1), 39–46.

BE THE CHANGE: CARDBOARD CONFESSIONALS

Artz, L. (2001). Critical ethnography for communication studies: Dialogue and social justice in service-learning. *Southern Journal of Communication*, 66(3), 239–250.

Frey, L. R., Pearce, W. B., Pollock, M. A., Artz, L., & Murphy, B. A. (1996). Looking for justice in all the wrong places: On a communication approach to social justice. *Communication Studies*, 47(1–2), 110–127.

Papa, W. H., Papa, M. J., Kandath, K. P., Worrell, T., & Muthuswamy, N. (2005). Dialectic of unity and fragmentation in feeding the homeless: Promoting social justice through communication. *Atlantic Journal of Communication*, 13(4), 242–271.

Rodino-Colocino, M. (2011). Getting to "not especially strange": Embracing participatory-advocacy communication research for social justice. *International Journal of Communication*, 5, 1699–1711.

APPENDIX A

SAMPLE INTRODUCTION TO COMMUNICATION STUDIES SYLLABUS

Instructor:
Office:
Phone:
Email:
Office Hours:

But in general it may be said that the things which we take for granted without inquiry or reflection are just the things which determine our conscious thinking and decide our conclusions.

—John Dewey, *Democracy and Education*, p. 22

REQUIRED TEXTS

O'Hair, D., Rubenstein, H., & Stewart, R. (2013). *A pocket guide to public speaking* (4th ed.). Boston, MA: Bedford/St. Martin's.

Warren, J. T., & Fassett, D. L. (2015). *Communication: A critical/cultural introduction* (2nd ed.). Thousand Oaks, CA: Sage.

GENERAL COURSE OBJECTIVES

In a complex and culturally diverse world, the ability to communicate effectively has become increasingly important. This course has two interrelated goals:

1. It will introduce you to the basic concepts, vocabulary, theories, and processes relevant to understanding oral communication in a variety of public and cultural contexts.
2. It will enhance your communication skills by providing systematic opportunities to practice clear, critical, and ethical oral communication.

Since it is our intent to integrate theory and practice throughout the course, your classroom experience will combine lectures, discussions, small group activities, written assignments, public speeches, and out-of-class observations. Together we will foster and maintain an interactive, open, and supportive classroom environment that promotes insight into self and others, critical thinking, intellectual growth, and communicative competence.

COURSE GOALS

- To understand and interpret public communication processes
- To develop inventional, organizational, and expressive skills
- To develop understanding and acceptance of communication ethics
- To develop critical skills appropriate for responsible receivership of messages
- To gain understanding of relationships between self, message, and others in public communication interactions
- To embody/enact communication behaviors that reflect each of the goals listed above

COURSE REQUIREMENTS

1. Three public speeches designed to increase your skill in creating, organizing, delivering, and interpreting informative and persuasive messages.

2. One communication analysis paper (five pages) designed to extend and apply course principles to a public speaking and/or intercultural communication situation the student has experienced.

3. Additional short, written reflection assignments and in-class activities/discussion to be assigned by the instructor.

4. Attendance and participation is an important part of your responsibility as a member of this class. Several written and oral assignments will be assigned and completed in class.

COURSE POLICIES

Grading:

To speak with me about a grade, please schedule an appointment. If you want to speak about a grade on a specific assignment, please wait at least 24 hours before contacting me. Grades will NOT be spoken about through email to avoid any miscommunications or FERPA issues. Please notify me regarding errors or discrepancies as soon as you see them. Keep all graded work to provide evidence of an error in the grade book.

Class Etiquette and Disruptions:

Respect and recognition of others in our class should be reflected and embodied by all within our classroom community. I will not hesitate to provide appropriate action to anyone who is communicating (in any fashion) disrespect, prejudice, or discrimination to others in our class and cultures outside of our class. I will not stand for speech that promotes sexism, racism, classism, or homophobia. If at any time you feel or experience someone else's discomfort with such issues, talk with me about it. In cases of class order and disruption (being any action or attempted action that negatively distracts or affects the class community, individual students, or the instructor), the following procedures will be followed:

1. I, as the instructor, will ask the student(s) causing the disruption to cease and desist.

2. I, as the instructor, will notify the disrupter(s) of possible suspension and/or dismissal from the class and of further possible classes.

3.   If disruption does not cease, I, as the instructor, will order the disrupter(s) out of the classroom and inform those involved that failure to do so will subject the disrupter(s) to student conduct sanction.

Attendance:

As members of a learning community, instructors and students agree to a tacit social contract. That contract ensures all participants will attend every class meeting, engage one another in an informed, spirited, and respectful manner, and complete all assigned responsibilities on time. Your instructor will begin taking official attendance in the second week of classes. You are allowed three (3) absences in the course of the semester. Each additional absence over the allotted three will reduce your final course grade by 5%. This means that eleven (11) absences is an automatic "F" for the course, even if you have done "A" work on all of your assignments. It is your student responsibility to ensure you appear on the attendance roster each day. NOTE: If you are late to class during speech days you will automatically be counted as absent.

Excused Absences:

The university recognizes certain events and obligations as "excused absences." You must notify your instructor prior to such absences with documentation from the sponsoring program or department, including contact information.

Electronic Devices:

With the rising ubiquity of technological use in the classroom (e.g., cellphones, iPads, and laptops), researchers have started to investigate the ways technology enhances/detracts from the learning process. Extant research has found that (1) taking notes via pen and paper results in better retention of information than taking notes on a laptop (Mueller & Oppenheimer, 2014); (2) students who refrain from using their cellphones during lecture/discussion take better notes and have greater information recall (Kuznekoff & Titsworth, 2013); and (3) laptop use during course lecture/discussion has a negative effect on the learning outcomes of both the user and those nearby (Sana, Weston, & Cepeda, 2013). Collectively, these studies show that unless you have a real and pressing need to use technology in the class (i.e., translator equipment for ELL students), using technology harms learning outcomes for you *and* your classmates.

TL;DR Version: If you don't need to use technology for classroom activities, then please refrain from using it during class.

Late Work:

Copies of all homework assignments and handouts will be made available to you (or someone you designate) to pick up after any class you miss. It is your responsibility to get and complete these assignments by the due date to receive full credit for the assignment. In general, no makeup speeches, exams, or written assignments will be allowed.

Writing:

Although this class focuses on oral communication, many assignments require that you report analyses of oral communication in a written format. For this reason, the quality of your writing matters and is part of the content of this course. While I do not expect you to be a perfect writer, your writing is part of what is evaluated. This evaluation includes assessments of organization, sentence structure, accurate word choice, typographical mistakes, spelling, and basic grammar errors in your writing. If you believe or we discover that you have trouble writing to the standards required for this course, please consider turning in rough drafts of your work well before assignment deadlines and/or consulting with a tutor at the Writing Center.

Email Etiquette:

Please keep a realistic time frame for expecting responses to emails. Expect most responses to be made within a 24-hour period during the school week and 48 hours during weekends/holidays. Emailing me an hour or two before class or any exam/assignment deadlines probably won't produce quick replies to urgent questions because I am most likely prepping for our class or other professional obligations.

Academic Dishonesty:

We welcome you to this classroom community with the assumption that the work you do will be your own. Distinguishing your work from the work of another, however, can be tricky at times—for both you and your instructor. You should know that presenting another's work as your own, even if through accident, is a serious violation of the Student Conduct Code. When in doubt, cite the source of the information. If you are uncertain whether you are citing sources sufficiently and appropriately enough to avoid plagiarism then please consult me or a tutor at the Writing Center.

Accessibility:

I strive to be conscious of and sensitive to disability issues. In the spirit of the Americans with Disabilities Act (ADA), I wish to make this course as accessible as possible to students with disabilities, temporary medical conditions, or mental or emotional health issues that may affect any aspect of course assignments or participation. I invite you to communicate with me at the beginning of the semester or at your discretion about any accommodations that will improve your experience of or access to the course. We can create an agreement to document accommodations and/or work with Disability Support Services to create an accommodation plan.

COURSE ASSIGNMENTS OVERVIEW

Informative Speech

What are your cultural backgrounds? How do they influence your way of seeing and being in the world? What does it mean to perform or "do" your identity? Remember the point is not to persuade us to be like you (e.g., a Democrat, a football player, a Christian, etc.), but to instead let us know what it means for you to communicate as (rather than about) your identity. The informative speech will be worth 100 points and should be 4 to 6 minutes long. A rubric will be given to help guide your preparation as well as detail my expectations for the performance.

Persuasion/Advocacy Speech

Despite the benefits that people living in a capitalist society might have, we have talked about some of the limitations of this system. Specifically, we have explored how neoliberal capitalism, as an economic and social system, may cause some problems or exacerbate others. In this speech, you should introduce your audience to one of these problems, provide multiple solutions, and then advocate for the solution you find would best address the situation. Things to remember: How do your cultural identities matter when talking about the subject? How does studying language help orient you in your understanding of the issue? How can you be a reflexive persuader of your topic? The persuasive speech will be worth 150 points and should be 4 to 6 minutes long. A rubric will be given to both help guide your preparation and detail my expectations for the performance.

Final Project/Speech

What is an issue or topic that you believe does not receive enough attention in your community or on campus? Tell us why it is important to examine. Be an advocate and motivate us to change our behaviors, attitudes, values, or beliefs. How do your cultural identities matter when talking about the subject? How do your audience's cultural identities matter when hearing your speech about the subject? How does language help orient you in your understanding of the issue? How can you be a reflexive persuader of your topic? This speech will be worth an overall 250 points, and may be 10 to 20 minutes long depending on the final speech/presentation assignment decision. You will work in groups of four or five members, to be selected through collaboration with me. A rubric will be given to help guide your preparation and to detail my expectations for the performance. Speech grades will include—but are not limited to—topic proposal, outline, performance, visual aids, and APA reference list.

Communication Analysis Paper

The goal of this paper is to examine a popular culture artifact (e.g., a movie, a show, a video game, a YouTube video) to understand its implicit messages. What I mean by "implicit messages" is that through the examination of your artifact you should argue the text achieves some communication goal. That process, however, should not be surface-level or obvious in meaning. For example, a paper arguing the *Fellowship of the Ring* is a text about the power of friendship in overcoming evil is not acceptable: It is obvious. After picking and watching the artifact ask yourself: What is this artifact trying to persuade me to do or believe? What is "normal" for the characters and does the artifact ask me to believe it is also normal? Why do I like or dislike this text so much and what does that say about how my identity is catered to (or not) through popular culture? The paper should be five pages in length and in MLA or APA format. The essay is worth 150 points.

Critical Chapter Discussions/Reflection Papers

You will be graded on participation in one of two ways: (1) You can contribute verbally during classroom discussion, or (2) you can TYPE two discussion questions derived from the reading and pass them out at the beginning of class. Typed questions should have three to five sentences of critique, reaction, or summarization of a text's argument and a one-sentence question or discussion prompt. Class participation will be graded as one of the following: 10 points (full credit), five points (half credit), or zero points (no credit). Verbal and written participation must exhibit familiarity with the text and a meaningful question, critique, or thought derived thereof. Simply talking will not constitute participation. Additionally, writing simplistic questions (e.g., What does X mean?) will not constitute participation.

GRADING POLICIES

Assignment	Points
Informative speech with final outline	100
Persuasive speech with final outline	150
Final speech with final outline	200
Any and all required visual aids and paperwork	50
Communication analysis paper	150
Participation	150
Total	**800 points**

APPENDIX B

SAMPLE PERSUASIVE SPEECH RUBRIC

(ADAPTED FROM THE NATIONAL COMMUNICATION ASSOCIATION RUBRIC)

Name:_____

_____ Instructor Score

_____ Peer Average (four student evaluations)

_____ Total

BASED ON NCA'S 8 PUBLIC SPEAKING COMPETENCIES	U	S	E	COMMENTS RELATED TO COMPETENCIES
Topic (narrow enough, appropriate, etc.) • Did you attempt to point out a problem that was directly related to capitalism? Did you use one of the organizational schemes from the book (e.g., Monroe's Motivated Sequence)?				
Thesis/Purpose (clearly reveals topic, previews, explains relationship to topic, etc.) • Attention-Getter • Thesis Statement • Preview of Main Points				
Supporting Material (adequate, cites sources appropriately, etc.) • Did you correctly and verbally cite four credible citations during your speech? • Did you use appropriate visual aids and give citational credit to any images, videos, etc.?				

Attention to the Speech's Purpose • Did you outline the economic dimensions of the problem? • Did you outline the governmental/legal dimensions of the problem? • Did you outline the communicative aspects of the problem?				
Organizational Pattern (appropriate, clear, logical, etc.) • Transitions • Fulfillment Statement, Review Statement • Concluding (Send-Off) Statement				
Vocal Qualities • Did you seem interested (not monotone) while presenting your speech? • Did you speak at an appropriate rate and have an appropriate volume to your voice?				
Pronunciation, Grammar, and Articulation • Could we understand everything you said? • Did you have proper articulation (not mumble)?				
Physical Behaviors (posture, use of space, eye contact, gestures, expressions, conversational delivery, dynamic, polished, etc.) • Did you speak in a conversational style? • Did you make eye contact with the audience (and not read from your notes or outline)?				

APPENDIX C

SAMPLE RUBRIC FOR COMMUNICATION ANALYSIS ESSAY

	EMERGING	E/D	DEVELOPING	D/P	PROFICIENT	P/A	ADVANCED
Introduction	1. Does not clearly show the "big picture" issue or exigency that the essay responds to. 2. Does not clearly show the necessity for the study's contribution to the audience 3. Does not have a clear thesis statement. 4. Does not have a clear preview statement.		1. Makes a vague claim for the "big picture" issue or exigency that reflects underdeveloped reading. 2. Makes a vague claim for the necessity for the study's contribution that reflects underdeveloped reading. 3. Thesis statement is present, but is either unclear or not reflected in the organization of the paper. 4. Preview statement is present, but is either unclear or not reflected in the organization of the paper.		1. Makes a clear claim for the "big picture" issue or exigency, but lacks sufficient evidence/reasoning. 2. Makes a clear claim for the necessity for the study's contribution, but lacks sufficient evidence/reasoning. 3. Thesis statement is present and clear, but not reflected in the organization of the paper. 4. Preview statement is present, and clear, but is not reflected in the organization of the paper.		1. Makes a clear claim for the issue, and is accompanied by strong evidence/reasoning. 2. Makes a clear claim for the necessity for the study's contribution, and is accompanied by strong evidence/reasoning. 3. Thesis statement is present, clear, and reflected in the paper's organization. 4. Preview statement is present, clear, and reflected in the paper's organization.

Text and Rationale	1. Does not demonstrate familiarity with the text's history. 2. Does not offer a succinct overview of the text's main plot points. 3. Does not clearly show the connection between the text and the "big picture" issue or exigency.	1. Demonstrates a superficial familiarity with the text's history. 2. Offers a superficial or overly detailed overview of the text's main plot points. 3. Hints at the connection between the text and the "big picture" issue or exigency, suggesting an unfamiliarity with literature.	1. Demonstrates familiarity with the text's history, but is missing an important development or source. 2. Offers a succinct overview of the text, but is missing an important plot point relevant to the essay. 3. Shows the utility of the text for the study, but could provide stronger logic/evidence.	1. Demonstrates a deep knowledge of the text's history. 2. Provides a succinct and compelling overview of all major components of the text. 3. Provides thorough support and evidence for the utility text to study the "big picture" issue or exigency.

(continued)

	EMERGING	E/D	DEVELOPING	D/P	PROFICIENT	P/A	ADVANCED
Effectiveness of Argument	1. Does not describe implicit messages of the text. 2. Does not provide specific examples from the text to evidence claims. 3. Does not provide a literature-based way to analyze the text (e.g., narrative, neo-Marxist, or feminist).		1. The arguments made only address obvious components of the text's communicative goals. 2. Provides few or unclear examples from the text to evidence claims. 3). Provide few or unclear literature concerning the analytical framework (e.g., narrative, neo-Marxist, or feminist).		1. The arguments made deal with implicit messages, but lack clarity. 2. Provides good examples in most places, but missing in others. 3. Provides an overview of the literature that contains small errors or misses important citations.		1. The arguments made deal with implicit messages, and the knowledge gained through the analysis is novel and clearly communicated. 2. Provides good examples from the text for all arguments. 3. Provides a thorough overview of the literature.

Organization and MLA/APA			
1. No clear topic sentence for paragraphs. 2. No clear transitions between paragraphs3. No clear signposting at the beginning of sections. 4. No clear transitions between sections. 5. Shows no evidence of familiarity with MLA/APA in-text citation, formatting, or reference citation.	1. Topic sentences only appear in a few paragraphs. 2. Transitions used only between some paragraphs. 3. Signposting present in some sections, but not in others. 4. Transitions used only between some sections. 5. Shows vague familiarity with MLA/APA in-text citation, formatting, or reference citation (e.g., mixes MLA and APA formatting rules).	1. Topic sentences are present, but do not always frame paragraph. 2. Transitions used between paragraphs, but some do not clearly connect the paragraphs. 3. Signposting is present, but does not touch on all the points presented in a section. 4. Transitions used between sections, but do not clearly bridge sections. 5. Shows familiarity with MLA/APA in-text citation, formatting, or reference citation, but makes serious and/or repeated errors.	1. Topic sentences are present and clearly connect to paragraph. 2. Transitions clearly and effectively used between paragraphs. 3. Signposting is present and clearly outlines all components of the text. 4. Transitions clearly and effectively used between sections. 5. Shows mastery with MLA/APA in-text citation, formatting, or reference citation, with only minor or few mistakes.

CPSIA information can be obtained
at www.ICGtesting.com
Printed in the USA
BVHW01s1532230218
508717BV00002B/146/P